*A Mother's Story of Unhitching from the
Roller Coaster of Her Son's Addiction*

Unhooked

ANNIE HIGHWATER

SIX DEGREES PUBLISHING GROUP
PORTLAND • OREGON • USA

Six Degrees Publishing Group, Inc.
5331 S.W. Macadam Avenue, Ste 248
Portland, OR 97239

ISBN: 978-1-942497-21-9
eBook ISBN: 978-1-942497-22-6
US Library of Congress PCN: 2016955160

Inquiries may be made by emailing
Permissions@SixDegreesPublishing.com

Cover Design & Editorial Oversight: Denise C. Williams

Author's note: This work is a memoir. I have written it under my pen name, Annie Highwater, to protect the privacy of individuals who are part of my story. Certain names, locations and identifying characteristics have been changed. Dialogue and events have been recreated from memory, and in some cases have been compressed to convey the substance of what was said or what occurred.

Publisher's note: While every effort has been made to verify web site addresses, the publisher is not responsible for broken links or addresses that have changed since this book was published.

Printed simultaneously in the USA,
the United Kingdom and Australia

www.SixDegreesPublishing.com

1 3 5 7 9 10 8 6 4 2

To my father, Jerry, in loving memory.
You were my first Corner Coach.

To Jeff, who always appeared when I felt I had no one.

And to anyone feeling alone in your struggle.

CONTENTS

CONTENTS

Foreword

I REMEMBER WHEN SHE CALLED ME, another mother desperate to save her son.

A contagious opiate epidemic has swept through the country like the devastating 14th-century plague known as the "Black Death." This year it has needlessly taken the lives of over 45,000 young adults. This book can be a guide of what to do when this contagious epidemic knocks at your door.

This epidemic is directly related to the marketing of opiate-based medications by drug companies and the over-prescribing of these types of deadly pills to the youth of our nation. The sad truth is, it isn't getting better, and most of the solutions people are coming up with do not work. Long-term treatment is the only thing that works.

Annie's story is not uncommon. I answered her call personally and have been part of her journey and fight to save her son's life. I commend her for having the courage to fight for her son's life and for not giving up, like so many do.

The road to becoming a heroin addict almost always starts with a pill. It only takes a little time for a person to become an addict and for the damage in the household to become irreparable. The good news is that we can win this fight if we just stay the course.

America's youth is worth fighting for and it must have a voice. Annie has now become this voice.

Greg Hannley
CEO/Founder
SOBA Recovery Center
Malibu, California

Introduction

Impossible is nothing. —Muhammad Ali

"*HELLO, my name is Elliot's Mom . . .*"
I am the mother of an addict. My son, Elliot, looks like a typical drug addict. He is the face of the common, everyday strung-out "junkie" of today. What does he look like? What you would expect to see in any middle-America suburb. Elliot is the all-American athlete, boy next door, with a bright smile. He's exceptionally charming with perfect manners for every situation. He's well loved, well-liked, well-known, well-dressed, well raised. He has the best sense of humor and a heart for stray animals that kept our house full of them. He spent most of his youth in private school and played baseball and football on elite traveling teams. He grew up going to summer camp and could be found in church youth group three times a week. He was a gifted athlete who could play Mozart by ear. He loved showing that off to girls. He could be your next-door neighbor or the catcher on any baseball team you see playing under the lights or the smiling football player you see

1

heading into the locker room, brushing off mud, pulling out his mouthpiece. He could be the friendly, smiling, approachable kid you see at the local mall.

He could be your son.

In his junior year of high school, Elliot suffered a jaw injury in football and was prescribed pain medication. That began a five-year descent into the darkest time of our lives. We'd had normal, individuating, teen issues up to this point—nothing diabolical. I was a single Mom but co-parented pretty well with Elliot's father and stepmother. Nothing yet had happened that we couldn't get handled with communication, consequences and firm boundaries. We had a nice little routine carved out for our lives, and it was working better than I'd hoped. But once addiction entered our picture, everything spiraled out of control so quickly and with such venom that I thought life would never calm down again.

∾

Finding out **your** child is drug addicted is similar to being kicked in the heart by a racehorse while you are barely awake, groggy, confused—and honestly didn't even know you were in the presence of a horse. Shock. Pain. Terror over every possible worst-case scenario. Bloodcurdling panic. Deep shame over what this says about you as a family, a mother, a father.

Often people feed that shame with their lack of understanding and fears. It is almost as if your problem is contagious—or caused by your assumed failures at home. This makes your misery that much more painful as it isolates you socially.

I had a strong temptation to beat myself to death with shame and blame. That, unfortunately, is what the addict plays on to manipulate you for sympathy and help. Addicts learn to sidestep accountability and remain in the addiction by blaming everyone else for what caused their behavior. Eventually that became of no importance to me as the urgency of the situation trumped every worry and argument of ego and as my knowledge of the tactics increased.

You want to hope that it's not true. How could it be? But it is. There is too much evidence that it is, in fact, happening—no way around that this is now reality. The torment overwhelms your mind. I felt like my blood had turned to mud and stopped flowing. The life we had known had ended. The strain of seeing my son decline into someone I didn't recognize was beyond painful. Terror entered our lives. That was when I started my fight—getting control of my mind and emotions so I could make strong decisions. I made up my mind we'd make it through this better than we went into it and that my son would not die or go to prison if there was anything I could do about it. My son was going to live and not die.

I went with Elliot on more than a five-year roller coaster ride. There were weeks at a time when I didn't know where my own child was living, who he was around and what he might be experiencing. It was excruciating. I was always jumping when the phone rang, especially during the night. It was a learning process, and I failed often out of ignorance or emotion. I wanted to believe in his sincerity, which doesn't exist when someone is in the throes of their addiction. Each time he returned to me, his tactics grew worse and I would have put him out again. It brought chaos and chaotic situations into my world, daily.

In the midst of all this, the most frequent statements expressed by others to me were:

- I don't know what to tell you;
- I don't *know* what you should do;
- I can't imagine what you are going through; and,
- I don't know how you are doing it.

Those four responses made my heart sink and my hope fall time and again.

Now, I'm able tell other people going through it:

- I *do* have answers—at least some steps you can take! I can speak hope and comfort, as one who knows;
- I *can* imagine, because I've been there. I have walked this terrifying road and came through to the other side; and,
- I can **help** you figure out how to do this! You are not alone.

I am telling my story to let others know: You are not alone. You are responsible for your own life, health, success and peace of mind; you just have to take the reins. The same goes for your struggling loved one. As hard as it is . . . don't hitch your peace of mind and well-being onto the roller coaster. Detach from it and work on your wellness. Learning that is the process of recovery. The healthier you get the better chance they will have of getting healthy. Finally, to let others know that as long as there's breath, there's **HOPE!**

~

What you are thinking you are becoming.
—Muhammad Ali

Non deficere. **Never give up.**
This is my story.

Addiction: Compulsive, physiological need for and use of a habit forming substance or activity.[1]

Co-Dependency: Excessive emotional or psychological reliance on a person.[2] [Typically one who requires support due to a disadvantage, illness or addiction.]

Dysfunction: Abnormality or impairment. A consequence of a practice or behavior pattern that undermines stability of a social system.[3]

Enabler: one that enables another to achieve an end; *especially* one who enables another to persist in self-destructive behavior (as substance abuse) by providing excuses or by making it possible to avoid the consequences of such behavior.[4]

Family: A basic social unit consisting of parents and children, considered as a group.[5] [May vary.]

Peace: Freedom from disturbance, war or violence. A state of security or order within a community. Wholeness, prosperity, tranquility, complete.[6]

Well-being: The state of being comfortable, happy or healthy.[7]

Opioids. In clinical settings, opioids are commonly used to manage acute pain, chronic pain and the pain caused by terminal illnesses. They work by causing the brain to produce large amounts of dopamine. Dopamine is partly responsible for the feeling of pleasure that you get from activities like exercise or eating a donut.

Opioids cause dopamine to flood the brain much faster than any natural experience. Our brains respond to this over-stimulation. Some parts of the brain responsible for taking in the dopamine die. When using an opioid like heroin, this can happen after just one use. The things that normally cause dopamine to be released and bring us pleasure no longer do. Opioids become the only pathway to pleasure and that is when addiction takes hold.[8]

ROUND ONE

Backstory: Burdens, Boxing & Books

*Once that bell rings, you're on your own. It's just you and
the other guy.* —Joe Louis

Synergeo: to put forth power together with and thereby to assist,
i.e., relating to negative or toxic components working together to
create positive, as with molecules of salt. Separated they are poison,
combined they work together for good use.[1]

GROWING UP THE YOUNGEST of six children was as difficult
as much as it was strengthening. Navigating my way through
a chaotic family dominated mostly by boys (I have one sister, four
brothers) wasn't easy for me, being a highly aware, often sick little
girl. The environment was hard for me—it was tough in general.
Life was never calm. I instinctively knew early on that I was not
a welcome addition. Sometimes it wasn't instinct at all —I was
outright told I was not wanted! We were poor and went without
just about everything.

My siblings teased me, "We're poor because you were born."
They said they had always had plenty to eat and even had pop in
the fridge before me. Now, having any type of soft drink was a

rare luxury. Many times when problems were surging, one or two of them would tell me it was proof that life had been good until I was born. I believed them, and it crushed me that I was the reason their lives were hard. It was immature sibling behavior that may not have been intended to do the damage it did. But my heart and soul absorbed every word, and it all took root deep within. I learned I had to be apologetic for existing and that I needed to serve or perform in order to be accepted. I learned to be loved meant I had to go "above and beyond" at all times in order for people to tolerate me. I also believed that anything bad that ever happened was always, in some way, my fault.

My parents' marriage was unhappy and fueled with arguments that went on for days. I never saw them laugh, hug, go out together, sit down to dinner together or enjoy each other. Never. Didn't happen. They seemed to have a partnership built on shared burdens and mutual misery. My mother retreated to the telephone, long naps and prescription medication. My father escaped into work, sports and self-help trends. I felt safer with Dad—my five siblings were closer to Mom. This was a house divided. My parents' struggles consumed them while the six of us were left to fight and figure things out for ourselves. I realized at a very young age that I needed to separate myself from everyone around me and search for answers myself when I felt confused or when things seemed off. I felt as though I had no one to lean on—each family member was busy managing their own suffering. I soothed myself by going off alone, apart from the noise and chaos. Sometimes, I would go outside and walk around the house, counting to a hundred over and over again.

To say growing up felt scary and unstable for me would be an understatement. Our house was always full of people and unending arguing—at least from my point of view. We moved several times and most of the homes we lived in were not big enough to hold a family of eight. My father was often sick and he switched jobs as we moved from house to house. I remember the terrors of the utilities being disconnected, the water shut off and going without food. We stood in line for boxes of free food at food pantries. I felt a sense of fear and shame from those experiences and that didn't leave me for decades. Then there were those times when finances would stabilize and we would do fine—life would almost get comfortable.

We actually lived in a couple of nice, large, new homes. But that lifestyle was never consistent and when, for whatever reason, the bottom would fall out, we seemed to go straight back to poverty level. I was fully aware of these things at an early age, and I envied families who didn't seem to have the scary burdens and chaos of our home life.

We attended many different types of churches, and in the process, we were exposed to all manner of people, which added to the confusion. Some of the settings were quiet and reserved, and others felt wild, odd and upsetting.

Through it all, nothing permanently calmed the suffering that was developing inside of me, but I found that I was able to find a level of relief and distraction in books. We often went without television or radio, due to whichever doctrine of church my parents were pursuing, but I could always have as many books to read as I wanted. My dad told me that the more well-read I became, the further I would be able to go in life. That sold me! I would pull away from group situations, sometimes climbing up in a tree or out in the woods behind our house. I would settle in, get comfortable and spend hours in my books. Losing myself in the rhythm of someone else's life on the page brought calm to my spirit more than anything I had ever experienced before. I dove headfirst into reading. I was never without something to read, sometimes having five books going at once. I took books to bed with me and I often carried a children's magazine borrowed from school to my dad's softball games. I would read and reread the stories, losing all sense of the sights and sounds around me.

Those early years were void of any discussion explaining life as it happened. When my great-grandmother died, I had to listen from the hall and try to figure out why everyone was upset and hurried. When I entered the room, everyone fell silent and shook their heads toward me. I interpreted that as something scary— something that I was to be excluded from knowing. I had to make up my own stories about most of whatever was going on in order to fill in the gaps of missing information.

Sitting alone on our back porch one summer day, my brother's friend sat down beside me and asked if I was excited about starting kindergarten. "What's kindergarten?" I asked. He told me it was to be my first year of school, and that I'd be starting in a few days, and that I would like it. I was aware my siblings were gone during the day, but my five-year-old brain hadn't realized that would eventually be expected of me! Having not been to preschool or any type of orientation, I was totally dumbfounded. I ran inside my house and demanded answers! That's when I was told we'd be going shopping for supplies and clothes. I was not excited—I was horrified and frustrated. This began the era of five-to-six years where communication, diligence and care for me were grossly neglected. Those years affected me permanently and I developed many quirks and issues of fear and defense deep within.

When I was seven years old, I became very sick and was quickly bedridden, which lasted for months. I developed pneumonia and my fever registered to the highest degree on the thermometer, leaving my parents unaware what my actual temperature was. I also had painful pleurisy and a throbbing ear infection. My parents were going through a faith healing phase, where they relied upon prayer instead medical attention, so they had stopped taking us for medical treatment. I slipped into a coma during the fever. I remember feeling half-awake. I remember people around my bed praying and crying. I had the sense that I was very heavy yet also very light, like floating in warm bath water. I remember wondering what I would do if my nose itched because my arms felt so heavy. I knew I couldn't lift my hand to scratch my nose if it did itch. I suddenly realized I couldn't sense my body enough to notice how my nose felt at all, so I told myself it must mean I would be okay.

My fever broke long enough for me to awaken fully. There was a terrible pain in my side from the pleurisy—it hurt too much to take full breaths. My ear was hot and felt as if it was exploding to the rhythm of my pulse. My parents rushed me to a church to meet with some men who were leaders to have me prayed over. As soon as they put hands on my forehead I threw up on the pastor's suit. Finally, I was taken to the doctor, where for days I had repeated injections of antibiotics. My mom and dad were told if they had they waited another day or two, I wouldn't have lived . . . and that my eardrum had burst. That ended the period of no medical attention for us. The sickness didn't leave my body for a long time. For years I felt weak, tired and small, and I never regained full hearing in that ear. But I was just happy to be feeling better. My mother made a bed for me on the couch so I could join the family again and I was given lots of coloring books and Popsicles. Those days spent recuperating and being cared for were, for me, a very happy time.

When I was well enough to return to school, I was told we would be moving, so I would be going to a new school and I would have a whole new life. But inside I was afraid to trust in the hope of that promise. I was sent off to my grandparents' house and brought home after the move was completed. I returned to a different home, in a different town and was dropped off the next morning at my brand-new school. My lack of understanding was overwhelming. Life felt dreamlike and blurry. I was still weak and struggling to adjust to so many changes. That many changes after an intense sickness seemed to increase my fear and misery. I withdrew mentally even more. In my new classroom, nothing felt real. Lights seemed too bright. The kids seemed louder than I remembered from my last school, and I felt smaller and even more separated by the burdens at home. Knowing I was uncared for always caused me to be highly self-aware and on guard—that awareness seemed even more glaring. The first three years at this school were also intensely dark, unhappy years at home.

Sometime during second grade, we had taken in a large litter of stray kittens who were sick and infested with fleas. I would sit at my desk in the classroom and watch fleas crawling from my socks, jumping onto other students. I was afraid to tell anyone the fleas were coming from me. Many times, I took my socks off in gym class to reveal dirty, black feet and legs so covered with fleas they looked like I had black, moving scabs all over them. Once I wore my winter coat to school that been soaked with cat urine. The school secretary had to call my mother to pick me up and have her take the coat from the coat rack after kids complained about the smell. Shame covered me like skin. Worthlessness began whispering to me.

The first time I visited the dentist was on a field trip with my class that year. My teacher noticed a brown spot across one of my front teeth. She tried to scrape it off with a butter knife! Once the dentist cleaned my teeth, he told us it wasn't a cavity; it was from drinking mostly cola and not brushing my teeth daily. The usual hot, acid wave of shame and embarrassment washed over me.

That school year, I went three months without being directed to take a bath or shower. I would scrub my skin with a musty, stiff washcloth that never left the bathroom sink so that I could feel clean. Instinctively, I knew I was dirty and it made me uncomfortable, but I was too young and ignorant to know how to care for myself. No one had taught me. Up until then, I was used to being told the bathtub was ready for me, but when life became hectic, no one seemed to prioritize things like that.

One night I sat in the bathtub after my bath until the water drained, waiting for my mother to return with a towel from the dryer, but she forgot. I waited and shivered until I was dry, which I actually thought was kind of neat. I sat analyzing the water spots as they shrank and dried around me. My father finally came. I remember the sadness in his eyes when he realized I had been sitting in the empty tub, wet and cold, waiting for over an hour. It hadn't occurred to me to get out on my own.

Neglect had reached new levels in that house. It was a very large, sprawling farmhouse, so it was possible to yell and not hear each other from one end to the other. Living there, I never seemed to be noticed or tended to. Those memories shaped my mind, and because of them, I later took obsessive care of my own child when he came along. I would often give him two baths a day, keeping him clean and tended to was my first priority. Because I had never felt cared for, I also developed an obsessive, lifelong routine of two showers a day myself.

I started questioning our family dynamics at this young age. To me, being frustrated and curious seemed the natural and obvious way to be. I was driven by the fact that I had been told and believed that I was the cause of all of our misery, therefore I should be the one to figure it out and fix it. I knew, very early on, there was a unique sadness over our home. There was a lot of mean-spiritedness and I felt a glaring void of love and kindness alongside the issues of poverty and neglect. I noticed how no one in our home laughed, hugged, or ever seemed happy and cared for. It was most noticeable when I saw other families and kids coming and going—whether at the grocery store, watching neighbors or observing people I saw in church. I was figuring out that our environment was not like any I had known so far.

I also realized that when I was with my grandparents, I felt different than I did at home. I felt relaxed there; I knew I was safe, taken care of and that they would talk *to me* instead of around or at me. I also felt confused by that as much as I felt safe enough to absolutely drain them of their attention and affection. I was dying for it. When they would send me back home, one of them would always remind me at the door that I was loved, that I was the "apple of their eye" and that I could become anything I wanted in life. They said those things so many times I would say them along with them! They often looked at me with a face full of sorrow as I left. I realized later that they were aware of the heartache and neglect going on at home.

I was growing more determined to find answers with every year. I wanted to figure out why there was so much unhappiness and chaos in our house. I thought that maybe if I figured it out, I would find that this wasn't all my fault. Then we would be happy— like they said they were before I came along. *Then I could be loved.* That was my plan. But I was never given straight answers.

My mother told me I was too sensitive and that she had way too many difficulties of her own to deal with yet another kid with problems. My father had more of a heart for my curiosity and tried to explain the general issues of life to me, as well as he understood them himself— usually based on a difficult experience he'd had or something from whatever book he was reading. He was limited by what he had come from himself, but he was trying. No one could tell me why our life was like this, nor why no one was doing anything to make life better. The confusion was as frustrating as my self-blame and all of the burdens themselves. We were all caught in the rhythm of this misery and affected by the burdens, as they kept on accumulating.

My dad made a difference in my life for years to come just by having those general conversations with me about life, usually on long car rides through the country. He told me I could be strong, regardless of how small and disadvantaged I was. He said I was smarter than most adults he knew. That one statement ignited a desire to actually *become smart*. He called me "moxie" or his "pistol" and told me what it meant to have grit and heart, despite size and disadvantage. He often used metaphors about boxing as a way of teaching me to face the hardest issues of life. Boxing was the common concept he applied in theory and advice over and again, cautioning me to never actually *physically* fight with anyone, if I could help it, but to approach life as a boxer in the ring. Boxers each have their own unique style and strength as much as their own personal set of fears and determination. He told me that in boxing, you shouldn't focus on odds against an underdog, it's more about the mind. I definitely related to the underdogs! I learned how important it is to find out as much as possible about your opponent. Their conflict style, striking ability, strengths, weaknesses, and the threat they pose, as well as their habits and strategies. That way, should the day come that you have no choice *but* to lock horns, you are well prepared.

At one point my dad enrolled us as a family in a kick boxing school. I hated every moment of it and very reluctantly earned my black belt. Getting up in front of a crowd for any type of performance, let alone one that involved possibly getting slapped in the face, triggered every fear within me. My sister ended up married to the teacher, so we were there all the time. Her husband started having me attend adult classes along with my youth sessions, singling me out to spar grown men instead of kids my age or size. For years I resented this. It wasn't long ago that I finally asked him why he was that tough on me. He replied, "Because you were small and scared. I knew you needed special coaching. If I put you against adults you were terrified of, if I stood you up against grown men who were three times your size instead of little girls, I knew, eventually, none of your peers would be a match for you. When you came back to the children's class you were so far advanced that almost none of the kids could handle you." I liked the theory, but I still would rather never be slapped in the face!

Fighting battles larger than my abilities and facing obstacles beyond myself would become a lifelong theme.

During those elementary years, I only found relief in spurts. I found comfort and answers in class story time and in the library of my school, along with boxing matches, but most of all, in solitude with books. Reading about other lives and places made me feel as if maybe someday I could have a new life . . . a life far away in an environment I could create myself, where I would feel welcome and safe. I could have as much love in my home as I wanted, and I could always be clean. One thing was certain: I knew that nothing around me was the way I wanted my life to be. In books, I found hope that someday this would all change. Someday my life was going be up to me. It would be *highly* functioning! And it would be calm.

I carried into my teens and through many adult years that old familiar sense that I was the most uncared for, unwanted, unwelcome person in every room. I never lost the sense that any bad thing that happened, happened because *I existed.* That core belief was the engine that drove every decision I made for years.

Whenever I overachieved, or when I grossly underachieved and gave up; whenever I fought back, or when I didn't react at all on my own behalf, whatever the situation was, my self-hatred and my sense that I was unwelcome and to blame were at the central core of all things.

I had no inner balance. The relentless screams in my mind from my home life followed me into every setting, experience and decision. I couldn't silence them. My burdens, my fears, and the sense of shame that I was carrying influenced all things.

∽

But what was meant for my harm . . . Gen. 50:20

Positive: All things work together for good eventually, if you allow them to. Later on down the road, many of those dynamics worked to serve me well when faced with the horrors of my son's addiction and all of the deception and dysfunction that comes with it.

- From leaning on my own intuition—versus how things appeared or what I was told—to standing on my own, scared and *alone* against what the crowd may be saying or hiding (people will become vicious to protect the monsters under their bed), the strengths I developed from childhood weakness were all necessary;
- Being the least welcome person in the room was fine with me when it came to dealing with the unsavory characters my son walked with on the path of addiction;.
- Books were a lifeline for me in my research for truth and how to handle boundaries, as much as my occasional escape from the madness of life; and, finally;
- Boxing proved to be my strategy of approach, viewing myself as the underdog fighting for the life of my

desperately addicted son against the opiates that would eventually hold him in a death grip. I studied everything about my adversary.

Good has come from it all. Strength came from *all* things in the long run, even the things I despised.

Annie's Message: I'm not trying to shame anyone, make anyone feel bad about themselves, or lead anyone to feel sorry for me. For the most part, people do the best they can with the tools that have. I went on to accomplish great things as much as to make terrible mistakes. I hold nothing against anyone, I blame the good and the bad of my life on no one but myself. Plenty of people have been through much worse! I simply hope to share my experiences. What happens in each of our lives can break you or fortify you . . . the decision is ours. What was meant for my harm, worked together with Synergeo perfection to fortify me. I forgive everyone and everything!

ROUND TWO

A Child is Born

Life doesn't run away from nobody. Life runs at people.
—Joe Frazier

Frustration: To break, make ineffectual, to shatter. To break apart literally, to interrupt, to disappoint, to bring to nothing; the act of disappointment.[1]
Rebellion: the action or process of resisting authority, control, or convention.[2]
Thanataphobia: The fear of death.[3] [The fear of losing someone you love.]

I MADE IT THROUGH ELEMENTARY and middle school, my frustration and misery growing like fire within. Life at home seemed to get weirder and more hectic by the year. I struggled terribly to fit in at school and get along with others, but it never seemed possible, I had too much inner torment. Everything felt threatening and fraudulent. After a while, we moved from the farmhouse to a smaller, newer home and things kind of became normal for a while. I had enough time there to calm down and settle into a routine—we had television again. At this age, I was

19

able to take care keeping myself clean and looked after. Hygiene became an obsession that I have to this day. This home felt safe and normal enough that I felt like I could invite friends over.

We were there less than two years.

After this house, we moved to an older home in the downtown part of my hometown. Issues of poverty and conflict returned, some worse than before. I was sick again often, missing school for one illness after another. We had a large, very old claw foot bathtub and no shower. Eight people taking baths on a daily basis was not easy to manage. Having become obsessed with cleanliness and hygiene at this point, I would get up extra early to get mine in first. Sometimes again running a bath later that night. I was not interested in ever feeling unclean again! I noticed that my parents argued more again in this house, mainly over finances and issues of faith or authority.

I had pretty much had it with my life by then, sinking internally into even deeper unhappiness. I hid it as much as possible, but fear and misery surged within me regardless. My mom got her driver's license at this point in her life and began driving my friends and me to school, the movies, the mall and so on. She became more active and present in my life at this time, but the neglect, poverty and years of not being talked to, taken care of or kept clean had taken their toll. The horror of being sent to school filthy and uncared for left me on guard and very sensitive to embarrassment. I still had not been given explanations about any of it. As a result, I never felt safe or relaxed and I was full of growing hostility. It was very difficult to have gone through all of that and then suddenly feel tended to, questioned or hyper-criticized by the one person I felt caused it all. The one person who I felt had disappointed, neglected and abandoned me more than anyone. I focused most of my pain on her. My mother was soft spoken, so most of my friends didn't understand how I could be so full of hatred for such a nice lady. I had no ability and really no desire to explain our history. Instead, I carried the torment of the memories and inconsistencies with me everywhere.

By the time I reached high school, I was *so* full of terror, insecurities, frustration and resentment that I found peace nowhere. My inner turmoil was turning into steady anger, cynicism and hostility. I didn't connect well or for long with my peers; I knew I was different. They all seemed to have calmer lives and cleaner homes. The stress I dealt with at home isolated me; I couldn't relax long enough to develop comfortable feelings anywhere. I did maintain a best friendship with a girl from elementary school and we are best friends still. I felt free with her, she knew how crazy my home life was for me, but she made me laugh about it. Around anyone else, no matter how I presented myself I felt like an injured animal. If anyone got too close to my pain, fear or shame I would either retreat or attack. Everything I did, said, or thought was coming from a shattered place. In order to adapt socially, I developed the ability to ridicule every situation, I used biting sarcasm as protective armor. Looking back, I realized many times that when I felt threatened, cornered by embarrassment or singled out, I would launch biting insults in order to try to cause others to feel how I felt. And normally, how I felt was ridiculed, ashamed, scared and exposed. But usually I just felt worthless.

The summer before I started high school, I felt comfortable enough with one friend that when she invited me to spend the weekend at her house, I stayed for the entire summer. I couldn't take my family stress anymore. My staying there was never discussed; her family just treated me like I belonged there, and they never made me go home. I never knew if they were aware of the hidden problems in my family, or if they were just that kind! Either way,

I sunk right into their family dynamic and absorbed as much of their normal family life as I could, I wanted to be swallowed up in it! It was a welcome relief. Her home was clean and didn't have the daily arguing and misery. I also considered my stay in her home to be a hiatus from all of the religious teachings I had never felt comfortable with. I was on break from the religious manipulating, ideologies and what I felt were absurdities that never seemed to make our lives any better.

During my summer in this family I could just *be*. No one was following me from room to room telling me that I "wasn't saved," or that I was "Unchristian" for normal, human behaviors that had nothing to do with issues of faith. I wasn't told that I "needed to repent," or that I was going to hell for this, that or whatever. In her home, it wasn't insisted that a bad day was a result of sin or Satan instead of just a bad day! And no one there hounded one another with the fearful predictions that the world was going to end in a matter of months. I made myself think about mundane daily things. I started to forget all that I was used to for a while. During this time, I had some peace.

I stayed with her until just before my freshman year. Starting a new school again was a struggle for me in every respect. My internal triggers were ever present. I smothered the torment by rebelling and spent a lot of time trying to find my way by playing drinking games with various friends. But I couldn't latch on for long anywhere or to anyone. Deep in my core, I believed I was too defective.

In my sophomore year of high school, by chance, I met a second person who would become a lifelong friend. Another relationship I consider to be compensation for what I lacked from family. This friend was a guy, but our friendship was genderless. He was sometimes my therapist, sometimes a mothering presence when life knocked me down and backed up over me. He was always on my side and quick with comic relief. That seemed to be a thread through any relationship and friendship of mine. A sort of gallows humor way of looking at the dysfunction I was surrounded by. I still hold a small handful of these friends close.

Near the end of high school, I found out I was unexpectedly pregnant by my first boyfriend. He was the only boy I brought close enough to me to completely see my home life. I was up front with him about the cast of characters and all of the stresses and embarrassment. He seemed unphased by any of it, even though he came from what seemed to be a normal family and lived in a nice, big, clean home. My polar opposite. It made me feel safe that he wasn't shocked and didn't see me as ruined or worthless. However, I was stunned by the pregnancy. I saw this young pregnancy as yet another embarrassing heartache. I hadn't been promiscuous; I hadn't ever really even dated anyone until him. That might have been different had I not had so many fears of connection and embarrassing elements I felt I needed to keep hidden. I was instantly filled with terror and despair about becoming a young mother knowing the family situation I came from. How in the world could I raise a normal, healthy child when I was so messed up? This wasn't my plan. My plan was to escape to a whole new life, away from my roots. A baby would trap me within them. All I knew to do was return to books. I began to read tons of self-help books and biographies about moms and families that seemed normal. My hope was that I would pick up new habits. I felt more and more at odds with my family, but by virtue of the circumstances, I would have to rely on them until I could get on my feet. Knowing the miserable way life had gone so far, I felt like I was drowning. I had little hope things would ever work out for me. I cried in my bed every night, miserable through the entire pregnancy. My relationship with Elliot's dad was young and dysfunctional, which added to my despair. I knew within a few months that I was forever locked in with someone I couldn't have a life with.

Elliot was born with bright blue eyes and strawberry blonde hair. I loved him so fast and so much that it filled my heart with pain. I was terrified to leave him alone with anyone that might be dysfunctional. I even insisted the nurses leave him in the room with me all night. I could hardly stand to have him out of my sight, I barely allowed anyone to hold him. My paranoia that someone might do something wrong and damage him permanently was overwhelming. I terrorized myself with this fear based on how I'd been mishandled and neglected. I wanted the complete opposite for this brand new, undamaged perfect little person. Sitting cross-legged in the hospital bed, leaning over his face I whispered promises over and over that I would never let him feel like I had. I promised I would protect him, I'd take care of him and keep him clean. I knew I desperately needed figure out how to be a mom. If necessary, I would fake it until I made it, so that he could have confidence and peace. I wanted this baby to grow up knowing he was loved, wanted and welcome in every room.

It was not an easy road.

~

Life is like a landscape. You live in the midst of it, but can describe it only from the vantage point of distance. —Charles Lindbergh

Elliot seemed to be an unusually active child. He didn't sleep through an entire night until he was almost two years old. I was never not exhausted and no method seemed to help for more than a night or two. He eventually worked it through on his own. Elliot took his first steps at just eight months old; he took them running from my arms to my dad's. It seemed like he never stopped running from that moment. Elliot wore me out chasing after him, day after day!

When he was five or six years old I found him in my parent's backyard, about fifteen feet up in a tree. When he saw that I'd spotted him he yelled, "Mom! CATCH me!" My heart stopped. One day I was laying out in the sun, reading a magazine while he spent forty-five minutes calculating precisely where he'd need to stand in the front yard in order to launch a water balloon over the roof of the house and land it just right on my forehead. (It exploded there perfectly—I chased him for fifteen minutes!) I asked everyone, "What am I going to do this kid?" He was like having a litter of puppies to chase after!

Elliot showed early cognitive and coordination gifts. When he was not even three years old, he pried open a makeup mirror with a screwdriver to pull the light bulb out of it and replace the one burned out in the refrigerator. My family still tells that story! When he was still in preschool, Elliot taught himself to throw a baseball up with one hand and swing the bat with the other; within days he was hitting the ball over the roof! He was so small and it was so astonishing to see that neighbors would sometimes line the fence to watch. They called him Baby Ruth. I was proud as much as I was nervous. My deep love and admiration for this child was always coupled with throbbing fears.

My relationship with my mother grew even worse through Elliot's early years. She was present in his life which meant over-involved in mine. She loved my child, but harassed my every decision. Her criticism of me for being too strict, too careful, too sullen, too tired . . . or whatever the case may be, was again met with sharp resentment considering how neglected I had been. It took me a long time to get into the rhythm of being a mother as it was being overwhelmed with misery and issues not yet worked through. She seemed driven to take over, amplifying the challenges. As much as I enjoyed the blossoming personality of this amazing little person, the threads of worry, misery and resentment along with that old familiar conflict were always present and surging. We struggled a lot—all of us.

Elliot's dad and I tried to make it work on and off for nine years, but we were both coming from too much brokenness. I thought I would cry forever that my son was suffering his first lifelong heartache because of me and my divorce. To make matters worse, my father died during the divorce process from a long-term heart problem that we had expected wouldn't take him for a few more years. During this time, a classmate of my son's was killed in a car accident. Not long after, a teacher was hit by a car in the school parking lot and killed in front of us. I saw unimaginable pain in the eyes of these families, and considering all things, I was starting to believe life might just always be impossibly cruel.

Once the shock of all of that settled, both of my grandmothers died within thirty days. I talked Elliot through all things as much as possible every single day. I soothed him and tried to explain to him that life would get better, terrible things were happening, but it wouldn't always feel like this. It was hard convincing him when I wasn't sure of any of that myself and our troubles seemed unending. But I knew I had to make life feel normal and safe for him as much as I could. I needed to become strong and resilient so Elliot could feel safe and become strong and resilient himself. Every sense was heightened; we became "easy bleeders."[4]

During these few years I decided I wouldn't die. I would keep on fighting, keep on swinging. I wouldn't turn to a person, place or thing to stop the hemorrhaging in my heart and keep my insides from falling out. I would do whatever it took to stay strong. I also made the decision then not to expose my son to a dating lifestyle. Not that there's anything wrong with it. I just knew we had more than enough on our plate and lots of work to do.

Instead, I decided I would set goals and make those our parallel projects as we got through the hard stuff. I started to run in the early morning or evenings and signed up for a 5K. I wanted our life to be normal and positive as far as what I could control. I took Elliot with me on training runs on his bike or scooter through the city. We had great conversations and spent such sweet time together during those outings. I decided to go all in and signed up to run a marathon. I had Elliot cross the finish line with me so that one day when he looked back on how we handled that season of loss and devastation, he would remember that accomplishment instead of a crazy environment, or a Mom losing control and turning to unhealthy types of support. I wanted Elliot to see that crushing loss and defeat does not have to send you into permanent dysfunction and despair—that you can set goals in the midst of terrible times and come out on the other side of them with rewards and results chasing you.

I was still drowning in decades-old misery during those years of drowning in misery, but too much had to be done every day to lay down in it for long. Along with goals and running, I also dove into church, thinking that would keep our life clean and safe, the two things I always chased. We were at church an average of four to five times a week on top of Elliot going to a Christian school during the day. I signed up for classes for myself, and I taught classes for Elliot's age group. There were also a few times I would get discouraged and overwhelmed, lose my cool, and go out with friends and blow it—further aggravating my patterns of self-loathing and overcompensating.

Running a race against misery and dysfunction is, to say the least, draining. But I kept after it! All I ever hoped for was a clean, safe, peaceful, boring life we could count on. Sometimes that felt just within reach.

It wasn't always misery and sorrow. When Elliot was ten years old, I saved enough money to take a vacation. It was the first vacation for both of us and our first time seeing the ocean. To say it was meaningful would not do justice to what that trip meant for us both. That week was one of the brightest, most joyful times of my entire life.

Annie's Message: Over time, without consistent communication or boundaries, you may become disenchanted and eventually be very angry, especially toward authority. I felt I was often reacting to frustrations and then hyper-criticized for my reactions to those frustrating things, while the frustrations were not resolved. The no-win feeling resulted in hopelessness and rebellion. I parlayed those my feelings into all of my decisions and then on into my parenting fears. I take full ownership of every area of my life, regardless what was said or done to contribute to my areas of misfortune. I forgive everyone and everything! Again, what happens in each of our lives can break you or fortify you . . . the decision is ours.

ROUND THREE

This Kid Though . . .

I want to be able to separate the average from the good from the great. I want to separate the ordinary from the extraordinary.
—Floyd Mayweather

Charisma: Compelling attractiveness or charm that can inspire devotion in others.[1] Special magnetic charm or appeal.[2] An undescribed magnetism that consistently draws people closer.[3]

SOME TIME PASSED. Elliot and I seemed to be settling into a comfortable routine following so much death, divorce and all of the other crises that took place around us. I worked very hard to purchase my first home. Life was centered around Elliot's school functions and ballgames. Things were calm enough during this time of life to experience some happiness. I continued to spend much of my free time studying and researching behavioral science and psychology, focusing on dysfunctional family patterns. I wanted to be as mentally healthy and strong as possible, so that Elliot had a fighting chance for a successful adult life. I constantly tried to come up with ways to create a Norman Rockwell-type of existence for him, despite any odds working against it. On the weekends he would visit his dad. I learned how to bake so he would come home to the cozy aroma of something in the oven. I thought it would be an instant comfort as well as a memory trigger in his future—he might one day smell warm apple pie and remember the comforts of mom and home.

It was obvious very quickly that Elliot's charismatic personality took center stage everywhere we went. He was developing athletic talent. Everywhere we went someone would come running, yelling "Elliot! Hi Elliot! Hi Elliot's Mom!" People stopped calling me by my first name. Elliot's Mom became what I answered to often how I introduced myself. We were settling into a very happy time. Elliot seemed to be the nicest, happiest, most gifted person in the world to me. I was beyond proud of my son, full of love and joyful excitement for the future. Family and friends would gather in the stands to watch him score game-winning home runs and touchdowns. Life was very pleasant. These years Elliot attended elementary and middle school at a private Christian school. I still struggled internally but was working very hard to provide a normal, peaceful life for him. I would call this a time of peace.

Our home life was light and happy, no major crisis, no major loss or conflicts. But outside our home life my relationship with my mother was boiling over with conflict and resentment. I couldn't escape her criticism. She would call me and then systematically send follow up emails and sometimes even written letters about things that were trivial with an urgency as though every concern was life-and-death. It could regard picture day. A sore throat, a shirt Elliot wanted. Being hyper-attentive, these were things I was already well aware of. I would beg, bargain and threaten to get her to back off, especially when it concerned harassing or upsetting me at work. Nothing stopped it.

One afternoon I was called into the human resources office, handed a printout of the call log for my phone extension and was questioned as to why my mom's number had made 133 incoming calls to my desk in the span of a week. I was flustered and humiliated, explaining to the staff member that she was calling to disagree about something my son was getting for Christmas. A relative was buying Elliot a guitar so he could learn to play and my mom felt I should convince them not to because a guitar would lead to rebellion. I apologized and told them I would address it. When I took the written record of the times and dates of her calls to her, she denied calling more than a handful of times. I reminded her that her "machine gun calling" when she was determined to make her point had been a daily argument between us and I put the evidence in her hands. She continued to insist that it had to be a company mistake. I wanted to tear my hair out. Nothing ever broke through.

There was no end to the arguments we had; all conversations ended with me pleading to be left alone and slamming down the phone or shutting my door to her. With all of the internal misery that lay dormant within me, I could not handle unending harassment from her. Many times our phone calls would even end with me shouting and calling her names. She would then call members of my family to tell them that I was out of control, and had been shouting . . . and calling her names. It was as if she would set me on fire and then call attention to my reaction as I was getting burned.

Once she called my work, home and cell phones in succession, over and again, to make a point on Elliot's behalf—a point that was not urgent nor anything that she needed to be involved with! After getting no response, she let herself into my home and came into the bathroom as I was in the shower. She wanted to let me know I was trapped and would finally have to listen. In a distressed voice, she rambled on that I may not be aware of stress Elliot had in school and that I needed to discuss his feelings with him, her finger pointing through the shower curtain. I burned alive on the inside, hot frustrated tears pouring from my eyes. When I turned the water off, she finally let herself out, saying she feared my temper. The frustration was relentless. It was insanity.

After Mom left, I sat Elliot down and asked him if he thought any of that was okay on the part of a grandmother. I then asked if he felt he and I had safe, open conversations or were they uncomfortable and closed communication. I knew we were comfortable and healthy; I just needed to be sure he did. Questioning his take on those things was my way of "bobbing and weaving" when these disruptions would happen. I had to fight back somehow, but standing toe-to-toe and out-talking her was useless. Eventually, I would be the one yelling, leading my mom to "tell on me" by calling each of my siblings.

Elliot acknowledged that our discussions were just fine and no, that was not at all normal, but it was kind of hilarious. It was hard to explain to him and help him fight the temptation to use her against any authority disputing him or daring to tell him no. He had a history of calling her with every complaint. If he'd been told no by me or his dad when asking for a gas station toy or candy bar, she would often show up later with it. Her involvement in our lives felt like a constant no-win situation. I wasn't strong enough to figure out how to cut her off and start over somewhere else. I was on my own with little resources. There was no working it through with her; we would never get to the bottom of it. As much as possible, I would work it through with him. All I could do was speak into the madness as it occurred and take care of the two of us as best I could.

Keeping my mother at bay as I enforced discipline and consequences was a fight that never took time off. She seemed determined to fight me for anything Elliot wanted. She would finish his homework assignments and sign him out of school if he had a test he wasn't prepared for. Every year I had to meet with his teachers a few weeks into the school year to have her contact with them restricted and make sure she was not permitted to sign him out of school. I usually waited until something was said to me once the school staff noticed issues of concern to them. I never felt that I would be believed on the merit of my word against hers. In my mind I assumed my mom would be believed over me, even though it was obvious to me who was telling the truth. I would return to the five-against-one battles so familiar when growing up with siblings—a dynamic that set the precedence of never expecting to come across as believable. Credibility had become a life-long apprehension. Since that is how it had always been in my family, I felt her version of the story would make me wrong, dishonest or even crazy for telling the truth. Year after year, school after school this issue presented itself. I wrestled worthlessness and credibility. These had become core issues of mine—one of those "shadow beliefs." I wasn't strong enough to stand on my own and say, "This is wrong and I demand boundaries." That strength came years later. Eventually, misery causes you to draw a line and say *"enough!"*

I worked two jobs during this time to keep Elliot in private school, to put braces on his teeth, and do anything possible to keep him from feeling as I did growing up—poor and uncared for. I wasn't aware that I was parenting him according to *my* needs, not his. I didn't understand why these things were not as meaningful to him. But I kept on, over-performing and working myself relentlessly hoping it was proof I was a good mother and that he was loved.

～

"There is more to a boy than what his mother sees. There is more

to a boy then what his father dreams. Inside every boy lies a heart that beats. And sometimes it screams, refusing to take defeat. And sometimes his father's dreams aren't big enough, and sometimes his mother's vision isn't long enough. And sometimes the boy has to dream his own dreams and break through the clouds with his own sunbeams." — Ben Behunin

Elliot's personality was undeniably charming. He had manners to a fault. He would often rush outside if he saw a neighbor carrying a trashcan to the curb or groceries from the car and do it for them. When I would go into his school, teachers and other kids would approach me and tell me he was their best friend, that he had the greatest manners, how he was their favorite. I loved and envied his ease with people. But his ornery antics continued at this age.

One morning I had just finished my hair and makeup for a work meeting, I turned on the kitchen sink to discover he'd taped the sink sprayer so it would spray my face when the water turned on, which it did. But it didn't end there. To top that off, getting into my car that same morning after fixing myself back up as much as I could, I started the car to find Elliot had set the radio on the loudest volume, turned on the windshield wipers and the blinker so I could be surprised again.

Spending an afternoon with a school friend, Elliot told the boy's dad, who was a pastor from our church, "My mom has gas problems," to make him laugh. (The pastor stopped to call from a pay phone to tell me, laughing so hard I could barely understand him.) Elliot's water balloon talent continued to be a thorn in my side. One afternoon he went home from school with a friend who lived a few streets over because I had a migraine. I stayed home from work and iced my head. Elliot was aware I was picking him up but not feeling well enough to get out of the car, so he was watching at the door for me. When I pulled up to the curb, I had my window down about four inches. With pinpoint accuracy, Elliot launched a water balloon from behind his back toward the car and somehow right through the window exploding it into my temple and all over me. I screamed so loud I think only dogs could hear. He was as ornery as he was taxing.

The older Elliot got, the more I started noticing he wasn't always using his humor and charisma with good intentions. Like the time one of his teachers called me into the high school for a conference to tell me that Elliot had missed some homework assignments because he had been doing too many chores around the house for me, including all of my laundry. I was asked to ease up on the work I expected of him. I thought my brain would explode! I always made sure he had chores to do and that he pitched in, but he wasn't overworked by any means and he certainly wasn't doing *my* laundry! I called Elliot over from across the large classroom and made him tell the truth! He admitted it was an excuse, but said he was intending it as a joke. His teacher didn't get angry, he laughed with him. I was furious. I lectured Elliot all the way home about character and honesty counting, even if you think what you are doing is just in fun. Elliot stared out the window laughing then said, "You know, Mom, you're really pretty when you're furious."

I knew I was in for some tough times in his teen years.

Annie's Message: While I believe it is important we remain vigilant that our kids are treated well, it does them no favors to favor them beyond consequences or to stand by as others do. More than anything my hope is that my son is healthy and loved and that his charisma is in balance with integrity and good character.

ROUND FOUR

Sucker Punches & Low Blows

Changing your nature is the hardest thing to do, but I discovered that you can be who you choose to be. —George Foreman

Conflict: To come into collision or disagreement, to fight or contend; do battle. A fight, battle or struggle, especially a prolonged struggle.[1]

Enmeshed: To wrap or tangle something or someone in a net.[2] To catch or entangle in, as if deeply enmeshed in a plot.[3] Unable to resolve a problem or escape from a bad situation. To entangle, ensnare, trap, involve.

Individuating: To give individuality to; to form into a distinct entity.[4]

Vicissitudes: A change of circumstances or fortune, typically one that is unwelcome or unpleasant.[5]

I STARTED NOTICING a difference in my relationship with Elliot in his last two high school years. Typically, we didn't have much conflict between us, unless it pertained to discipline and normal frustrations—on both parts. Bad moods, bad days, what have you. But later in his high school career, I started catching onto different types of behaviors. Because I was always on high alert to avoid being dysfunctional, I researched and studied everything as it occurred. I constantly sought professional counsel; I didn't trust myself alone on major decisions. I just didn't have the confidence and felt I didn't always have strong knowledge either. I second-guessed everything because of my background. I continued to study how to live as clean a life as possible. I was afraid to even swear or have music play in my home that included foul language. I was full of anxiety.

I called a friend—a psychologist who worked with teens at a youth center—with my concerns. From her I learned the concept "individuating." Almost all teens will go through a mental and emotional separation from their parents in preparation to become adults, move on from their home and go out on their own. But this felt different, this was not just separating and growing pains. What I was sensing in my son felt more secretive and sinister. Since I felt I had gone out of my way to create an environment in my home that was clean, healthy and sane, I was naively hurt over these changes. Because I felt I had been careful to not take my dysfunctional background out on him or act it out in front *of* him, I took this phase he was going through extremely personal. I saw it as a personal failure. I thought I had done all the right things to prevent teenage rebellion. The fact that my son would even entertain dishonesty or do anything negative or wild felt like betrayal!

Once again, I felt defective. Looking back I felt foolish and selfish for making so much that happened about my own inadequacies.

When Elliot was a new driver, he approached me to ask if he could start going to a teen nightclub with his friends from school. They were "*all* allowed to go!" he claimed. He was careful to name only the friends that were known for *not* getting into trouble. He rattled off a list: athletes, kids from church and even threw in a buddy who was planning to study pre-med! "Only the well-behaved, well-parented, angelic kids go to that teen spot." I was onto that trick though. I knew as a parent and having been a teenager myself that the stronger the sales pitch, the less I could trust a situation.

My feeling about letting him go was "absolutely not." Not only because I had a feeling he was working me over, but the strongest reason I wasn't going for it was that I didn't want him making the twenty-five-minute drive. I knew the location of the club. He would be traveling on three different freeways with his friends. It occurred to me that they were also inexperienced drivers, and they might possibly drive while under the influence of drugs or alcohol. I told him I felt that a group of kids gathering was fine as long as it was in a safe, healthy environment closer to home.

Not more than a few weeks later, I overheard him talking about "Foam Night" in a manner as if he was planning to attend. I was furious, but kept it to myself not wanting to pounce on him in a conversation I wasn't sure of. When the date for Foam Night rolled around, Elliot asked me if he could meet some of the football players at a girlfriend's house to watch a movie. He said no one was going to Foam Night after all. I told him that was fine, yet intuitively, I knew in my gut he was going to try something devious. I decided to trust Elliot, let him leave the house and deal with whatever happened, **if** it happened. I felt that I couldn't prevent every misbehavior; I could only deal with it once it had occurred. But I was on high alert!

About an hour and a half after Elliot left, he called me from his cell phone to check in. I asked him to call me again, but from the girl's house phone where they were watching the movie. He fell silent for a moment and then responded, "Yeah, give me a few minutes."

It was a Sunday evening and I was reading a book in pajamas that had cows and hearts patterns and said "Love Me" all over them. My hair was piled high on my head, my contact lenses out, glasses on, and no makeup. I was not glamorous or even presentable the public! But I knew I had no choice. I knew based on what I'd overheard and suspected, judging by the way he acted and the fact that he couldn't call me immediately from that home phone meant that he was probably actually *at* Foam Night! I was boiling. Changing nothing about how I looked and was dressed, I got in my car and raced up those three freeways to find him. As I was walking in, I passed a few of his buddies and asked one how long Elliot had been gone. I phrased it that way intentionally instead of asking if he had been there so I would come across as if I already knew he was there. That way it wouldn't give the boy a chance to lie and cover for Elliot. He told me Elliot had left about ten minutes before.

I figured he was must be racing back home right about then.

I marched on in and made my way through the club, walking through in those "Love Me" cow pajamas, and spotted the deejay booth. I saw several of his friends on the way to it, each stopping to stare. I was not sure if it was because Elliot's Mom was at Foam Night, or if it was because I was in the pajamas, glasses and had my hair in a big messy bun. They usually saw me dressed for work. I made sure to ask any friends I recognized if they'd please let Elliot know I was looking for him, even though I knew he had left. I wanted embarrassment to be a package deal along with any other consequences for such a huge disobedience. I reached the deejay booth and passed through the mountains of foam and dancing teenagers. I asked the deejay if he would please have my son paged because he wasn't supposed to be there but had tricked me and come anyway. The deejay looked irritated by that and told me that it happens often. He paged Elliot at least thirty times. Interrupting the music to announce "Elliot! Your mom is here . . . Elliot you are *not* allowed to be here. Attention Elliot please come to the deejay stand, your mom is here for you!"

As I was standing there my phone rang, it was Elliot calling to tell me he was at his cousin's house and . . . where was I? He said all he could hear was music and a deejay, like I was in a bar. I let him know I was at Foam Night and to meet me at home. I told him to get comfortable because he wouldn't be leaving the house anytime soon. "Okay," was his only response.

That was a memory I hoped Elliot would take into his adult years, knowing I would go to extremes to keep him safe and to make sure he obeyed rules. Being a single mom, alone in a home to manage an extremely strong-willed boy, I felt I had to set the bar high and come through strong with consequences. His safety depended on it. His future and his life depended on it. Disobedience can get you killed.

Elliot was furious for a long time. We've just now got to a point where we can laugh about that night. Foam Night was the first of a few times I went down the rabbit hole *with* my son. At times I participated in the madness with him, even though I was at the opposite end of it.

While that may be a funny story and many of may have prevented him from going again (or maybe not!), I wouldn't recommend pursuing your child that way. I don't know that I would do all of that over again if faced with some of the situations Elliot created. While Foam Night may have been amusing once my rage dissipated, the next few years involved many incidents that were upsetting and scary. I can't say I handled them all with wisdom.

After Foam Night, one thing was for sure: I trusted nothing.

At this point, I knew I needed to be completely in my child's business. I pulled his phone from his room when he was sleeping and went through his texts, finding conversations about being out all night one of the few times I'd let him sleep over with a friend. It may have seemed extreme, but after everything we'd been through and as careful as I felt I needed to be raising Elliot, I didn't feel that all-night sleep overs were always a good thing, unless I was familiar with the standards of the family and who all might come and go from the home. I felt my heart fall when I read that he'd been up to much more than I expected.

Going through Elliot's phone and social media, I also found messages with terms I hadn't heard before. I wrote them down and called a police officer I had known for years, confirming my worst fears about hard partying and drug experimentation. I decided to gather as much information as possible and then let Elliot know he was going on total lockdown and it was not just because of Foam Night.

Elliot's reaction when I laid it all out to him at first was anger and embarrassment, but then turned to relief. It was as if he'd been hoping to be caught and reeled in—and I was glad to take the reins a little tighter. He seemed to settle in quickly and adapt to a quiet, structured life of home, school, church, sports and not much beyond.

During this time of lockdown, I worked hard and saved enough to take Elliot on a cruise to Jamaica for a senior year gift. We had an amazing vacation. To this day it is still one of the best times of my life to look back on.

We battled here and there once we returned from Jamaica throughout that winter, but it was nothing earth-shattering. I had lots hope. During those months, Elliot had sustained a jaw injury while playing sports that needed to be looked at by a surgeon. In private, I pleaded with the doctor not to prescribe him narcotic painkillers, letting him know we come from a family riddled with addiction. However, despite my concerns, Elliot was prescribed narcotic pain relievers. It was no more than a matter of days when chaos erupted and kicked into overdrive. Within a few weeks I found pill bottles with my mother's name on them hidden in Elliot's bedroom. She denied that he had access to them; he claimed she gave them to him. I was never able to get to the truth. I thought once I addressed the misuse and sharing of pills and once the prescriptions ran out, the problem would be handled. I wasn't prepared for the nightmare it would all eventually turn into.

～

I remember when I lost my mind. There was something so pleasant about that place. Even your emotions had an echo in so much space. —Gnarls Barkley

Elliot turned eighteen that year and was pressuring me for permission to drive to Florida with a caravan of friends for spring break. For all my usual reasons, my response was, "*Absolutely not.*" Given our painful history, especially a long car ride with a group of teenagers, I knew there may be binge drinking (probably along the way as well as during the whole week). It was not something I wanted to allow my only son anywhere near.

The trip became a daily dispute for three months. Elliot argued, begged and bargained constantly. He was relentless, even involving my mom to plead his case. My answer was final; their onslaught miserable. We had reached a deadlock and I let him know in one final conversation, "Elliot you are eighteen years old. If you choose to take this trip, it is your choice; however, I will respond to your decision. You will not be on my cell phone plan; you will no longer have your vehicle to drive when you return. Nor will you return to this home; you are eighteen. You can stay with friends or your grandmother if you betray my decision this time. The decision is yours." Elliot agreed with frustration and eventually seemed to make peace with my final answer. The conversation was not brought up again.

When April rolled around, I walked in the door after work on a Friday afternoon after a long week. Setting my stuff down, I found Elliot waiting for me in our living room. Smiling and happy to see him, I asked if he'd had a good day. Elliot said, "Yes I did! Now I have a question for *you*. Remember how you told me if I chose to go to spring break with my friends I wouldn't have a phone, a vehicle or home to return to?"

My stomach started to sink. "Yes, of course I remember. Why?"

Elliot said, "Well . . . it's worth it. My ride is about to be here, my bags are packed and I'm going to spring break. Call Grandma if you're upset; she's known the whole time I've been planning to go. She agrees with me that I should get to do this."

Again, my mother was grossly enmeshed in our lives. I wanted to throw up.

My counterpunch was turning Elliot's phone off before he was out of the neighborhood. I then began a seven-day vigil waiting for his return, praying for his safety and battling my mind against all the dreadful things it tried to tell me could happen to my son.

I also spent the week bitterly arguing with my mother who would not budge and admit any involvement of hers was wrong and boundaryless. Sick to my stomach, I went to work every day unable to eat. I texted Elliot's friends a daily countdown to their return every day as reminders to him that the week was temporary, but coming back to the consequences would be permanent. I wanted my son to learn from this that the impulse was not worth the brief gratification in the long run. When Elliot returned, he stayed with my mother for a month and went to school from there, but unable to tolerate the loud, dysfunctional environment of her home, apologized and earned his way back into mine. This was the beginning of the gut-wrenching cycle of Elliot defying household rules. I would force consequences, tell my son to leave and have him return weeks or months later roughed up by his living arrangements and extremely, albeit temporarily, contrite.

～

Elliot graduated high school a few months later despite the troubles he was having. In the weeks leading up to his graduation party, I started noticing money and items missing from our home. The conflicts between us were increasing and making a lot less sense. I received a call from my mother one evening to tell me Elliot had hidden an addiction to painkillers from me ever since the first prescription was written. She said it had control now and they needed me to know. She told me she had known for a while. I felt like I'd pass out. I lowered myself to my knees to keep from falling. I sat on the floor for a long time with the disconnected phone in my hand and let my mind turn in circles.

I canceled his graduation party and spent the next month putting him out, taking him in and fighting my way through despair. Twice I sat up all night beside his bed trying to detox him myself. In my spare time, I tormented myself with blame and fear and tore my hair out over what in the world to do.

Going to work during the day and maintaining a level of professionalism was just about unbearable. I kicked it into autopilot, and most evenings I came home and fell apart. It was painful to sit in meetings and listen to corporate concepts that could no longer feel important. Hearing the minor complaints from people about their kids or their mother became unbearable. Hearing normal milestones of my coworker's kids felt like swallowing a hot brick.

Some days, I felt as though there was no life in my legs—I was walking from place to place through quicksand.

Annie's Message: I don't understand many of the decisions that others made. Decisions that seemed to harm and hinder more than help. I have come to understand than when someone believes they are helping, even though it's an unhealthy helping, they are blind to this. Their obsession with being the one coming to the rescue overrules logic. There is usually no getting through when someone is an enabler on that level. Again, I hold nothing against anyone. Most often people do they best that they can with the tools that they have. I choose to forgive and move forward. Sometimes forgiveness means renovating a relationship; sometimes it means no further contact. Either way, in my opinion, forgiveness is the best way to heal and have hope for a great life.

ROUND FIVE

Stepping Into the Ring

Before I fight I always pray that no one gets hurt.
—Sugar Ray Leonard

Obsess: To occupy the mind excessively.[1]
Persevere: To maintain purpose in spite of difficulty, obstacles or discouragement, continue steadfastly. To persist in speech, interrogation or argument; to insist.[2]
Ruminate: "Chew the cud" compulsively focusing attention upon the symptoms of one's distress. Mull over, deliberate about, puzzle over.[3]

NOT TAKING THE NEWS LIGHTLY by any means, I set my resolve to go on a crash course to learn exactly what I was dealing with. By virtue of being a student of adversity as much as a fighter, I went on a mission to learn from as many sources as I could find. Beginning with Nar-Anon groups, drug and alcohol counselors, family therapists, pharmacists, doctors, teachers and school administrators, and police officers familiar with trending drug problems. I also tracked down those I call the actual experts: drug dealers, addicts and recovering addicts along with their affected family members. I would literally interview them with my list of nonthreatening, nonjudgmental questions. I was on the hunt for information about opiates, heroin and the effects of that type of dependency on the addict and those involved with them. I planned to arm myself with knowledge and information so I could handle my son as correctly as possible.

I returned to my dad's boxing metaphors for encouragement and decided I would view the crisis that had entered our life as my contender. I needed to know everything possible about the opponent and I needed to come up with a strategy for battle. I started keeping notes and journaling the daily experiences, along with failures, accomplishments and any strategies for coping, handling and responding that seemed to help. Daily, I would read, hear or come across something someone had experienced that helped them overcome painkiller addiction. Each time I quickly added each pearl of wisdom to my notes.

I remained in Elliot's business at all times, within safety and reason. Sometimes I crossed those lines. To say I was obsessed would be the greatest understatement of my life. Besides, I was still a mom—and a mom living in horror at that. I snooped constantly, I made myself *crazy* snooping! I nearly always found bad news and new terrifying details about my son and his friends. Some of these kids I had known since little league or his elementary years in a Christian school. It was like discovering a secret underworld where people you know are the secret members. It was shocking. If I came across a new name, I ran every type of background search possible on that person and any one of their relatives or associates I could connect to them. I left no stone unturned. I was consumed!

~

I come as one, but I stand as 10,000. —Maya Angelou

I was seeing a side of life that I could barely stand to imagine my son was involved in. And "Elliot's Mom" was becoming widely known in that world as well. It was common for me to return text messages meant for him from his phone or reply from his social media when I saw familiar characters or recognized code words I'd learned stood for certain drugs. One response I used regularly was "Hi! Actually, this is not Elliot; it's Elliot's *Mom*. How are you? *Sooo* . . . I will be at your front door with a narcotics officer if you contact my son regarding pills or illegal drugs again."

That was my typical counter-punch. I was normally a defending fighter more than someone who aggressively charged with a strong offense. But as time went on and situations became more frightening, my fighting style became more like a wound up, out of control brute running into the ring to fight for territory.

Several times, I followed Elliot into pawnshops to buy back my own things. I also began following him into scary neighborhoods, street after street filled with condemned, boarded up homes. My fear for his life outweighed any fear for my own. A handful of times, dressed up for work I would knock on the door of a home on one of these streets after watching his transaction. My son looked thin and frail. It pained me deeply to see him hand over money and stuff whatever they gave him in return into his pocket. My heart burned alive every time.

After he would drive off, I'd take a deep breath and approach the door. I politely let whoever opened it know who I was. "I'm Elliot's Mom." I forced calm into my voice and told them I planned to set camping gear up in the yard and call attention to all of us with a quick call on speed dial to my friends at the local TV news station if Elliot was ever seen at their door again. I knew I had to threaten something different than anything they were used to. Often seeing guns and intimidations tactics as soon as the doors opened, I knew any attempt of mine to threaten or intimidate would be laughable. And it would probably get me hurt. I used exposure and my connections to media and police as my threat. I figured it may keep us safe if any of these dealers felt involvement with Elliot, as well as assaulting his mother for approaching would result in news vans and patrol cars in the front yard. When you are operating criminally, you normally prefer to keep it in the dark. Threatening to shine a big spotlight was all I had. So that is exactly what I told them would happen. I spoke strong and bold, as if I had no doubt. Time and again I used this threat to disarm people who would normally cause me to be petrified of. Somehow it worked every time.

My bolo punch tactics were effective, however, they always caused strife between Elliot and me—but it was worth it. I considered it collateral damage. Our relationship could return to peaceful when he was healthy. And, if necessary, I would apologize later. For the time being, I believed I was in the fight of my life— for his life. SO, I would do whatever I had to do, even if it meant making him furious with me.

His backlash told me I was shaking things up and achieving my goal of not making it easy for him. I wanted that path to be absolutely miserable. Miraculously I was never hurt or even threatened in those encounters. Twice I vomited beside my car right after and then drove on into work, pretending all day in front of clients that I was as composed and professional as normal. Elliot would call not even an hour later screaming for me to stay out of his life and not to ever again go near his "friends."

I interpreted those reactions as victory. I was doing things as crazy as my son was and I wasn't even high.

Anytime I faced intimidating people or places, I would repeat the quote, "I come as one, but I stand as 10,000" to bolster myself.

I would imagine the strength of my dad, standing tall behind me. His eyes as blue and fierce as they were anytime I saw him face a threat. I would then stand a little taller and believe I was not fighting as one, I stood in the strength of 10,000. I told myself that I had fighting spirit of my father and an army of champions resident deep, down on the inside of me and then I would come to believe it.

I would never advise anyone do anything like that. But . . . I was a frantic, fear crazed Mom on a mission to see my only child through to the other side of a nightmare. A nightmare he seemed to prefer. I lived in terror and that terror was transforming me into an almost fearless brawler. Elliot's outcome was my priority. I only saw two possible scenarios. This would be a success story or it would end in tragedy. I never lost my focus on those outcomes; they governed every decision I made—including agonizing ones like shutting my door to him when he had nowhere to go but was refusing my offer to take him to treatment. I forced myself to not help or enable him, giving him nothing except an invitation to treatment. We volleyed back and forth between silence and volcanic eruptions of chaos and turmoil. It was one extreme or the other—no gray area.

Our standoffs were torture. Long-term stress can take a toll in many ways. One of the worst things we endure in a crisis is waiting: waiting for things to move, come to a head or change. You feel like you are absolutely stuck in the mud. When the stakes are high and terrifying, it will send you into mental torment like nothing else. Being "in the meantime" is where the struggle was the hardest for me. At least when a crisis would erupt I would know what was going on and where things were heading.

In the quiet, in-between times, you go to battle in your own head wondering, most often through the long, silent nights.

~

Courage is not simply one of the virtues, but the form of every virtue at the testing point. —C.S. Lewis

During these times of "Limbo," I would create coping methods to console and distract myself through the night. The best of these were writing, yoga, meditation and prayer, which settled my mind and made me feel as though I was playing a part in influencing the outcome. I believed and prayed for positive outcomes, speaking the prayers aloud when I was alone. Sometimes in Elliot's bedroom I would whisper, "This will end well, this will end well . . . and this will end *soon*." Whenever I saw any sign of progress or proof, my faith boosted me and I could go on much longer.

The grief was crushing me. The sense of dread over the situation would never leave me; sorrow and fear hung over me like damp, dark clouds, but I was able to find temporary peace and distraction, rather than burning alive on the inside around the clock. I could figure no way of getting out of my miserableness. But I would *not* be unproductive! In between crisis, chaos and meltdowns, I took all of my angst and the energy created by it and put it to work. I knew I need to fill those in-between times or I might permanently snap.

When I had time off work, I added miles to my bike and running routes, sometimes driving to other cities to run five or ten miles through different scenery, but always checking my phone for calls or texts! But hey, at least I was doing *something* instead of driving around looking for Elliot or lying on my floor at home, obsessing about what was going on with him. I stayed vigilant, firm in my boundaries and as busy as possible. I attended behavioral science classes and signed up for several local races. I spent hours studying the root meanings of words, clichés and cultural concepts that felt meaningful to the situation. Anything gave me hope if it related to the pain and fear I carried.

I also started going to weekly therapy for my own well-being. I confided in a coworker, who had a very kind, compassionate personality. Her support for me got me through many days in a busy office when my mind was everywhere else. She ran interference for me with my clients if she sensed my anxiety was reaching desperate levels. At the same time, I grew close to an older woman who worked in the court system and counseled families in crisis caused by dysfunction or drug/alcohol abuse. She was the first person I had allowed to be anything close to a mother figure for me. I had struggled with trusting women all my life.

These two phenomenal women became life support.

Annie's Message: Taking care of yourself on a daily basis, as much as you can remember to while in times of crisis is absolutely crucial. Especially when exposed to long term stress. Remaining safe is even more important!

ROUND SIX

Glass Jaw

My strength is my weakness and my weakness is my strength.
—Boom Boom Mancini

Chaos: Complete disorder and confusion. Behavior so unpredictable as to appear random.[1]
Misery: A state or feeling of great distress or discomfort, of mind or body. Unhappiness, distress, anguish, anxiety, torment, pain, grief, fear, heartbreak, despair, depression, gloom, sorrow.[2]

THERE IS NO PERFECT WAY to describe the insanity that we were all experiencing, including Elliot. I had no clear plan for what to do and everything seemed to be getting worse—from my relationships within my family to the issues Elliot seemed to be constantly creating. Apparently, our family dynamic was just never going to work, no matter how I tried, no matter how talented, charismatic or amazing Elliot was. The clean, calm household, the baking every time he came home, private school, piano lessons, sports involvement, mentors, church—none of it mattered anymore. No matter how I plotted, studied, begged, pleaded, performed or stood my ground, nothing would level out our life.

We were undeniably a mess.

~

There is no coming to consciousness without pain. —Carl Jung

I went to church alone every Wednesday and Sunday, sometimes quietly whispering a prayer request to a leader. But I was so consumed with fear, shame and pain that I never gave much detail. I simply asked for prayer for "a personal situation." I . . . *we* . . . needed help. I knew I needed a strong team if I was going to fight this, and I realized had to start building one and exposing our truth to at least some degree.

I met with Elliot's youth leaders, teachers and administrators. I called parents and coaches. No one had one set method or idea. I called the parents of any kid whose name I found in conversations linked to drug use, whether I had overheard them, or had found messages in his phone or on social media and let them know of my suspicions. Most of them were teammates from baseball and football, so I was familiar with each family. If I saw even a hint of drug terminology, I reached out to let the parent know their child may be involved in the recreational abuse of prescription medication along with mine. I would call them and say, "I don't know if you're aware and you don't care, or you're not aware at all, but if I found out you had this information about my son, as dangerous as it is, I would be knocking at your door demanding to know why you didn't contact me immediately. So I'm contacting you now to tell you this is what is going on with our kids. Do whatever you feel is best with the information."

I would then let them know I had proof and evidence that their son or daughter was involved in the misuse of painkillers. Shockingly, I was often met with anger and condemnation. I usually found that the parents didn't want to believe it, didn't want to deal with it, or they had their own demons to hide. One parent told me their son, who I knew was actively involved in snorting pills with my son, was "only spending time with Elliot to be a good influence on him. Because Elliot was being raised by a single mother and their son felt sorry for him." I couldn't believe it. That felt like a shotgun blast to the heart.

When I reached out to another father, he threw up his hands and angrily said to me, "What are *we* supposed to do? Boys will be boys!"

I couldn't give up so easily. I refused to minimize the situation or deny it. I had to cut my losses as I went along, and I told myself *I'm not doing any of this to make friends.*

As I reached out to people, the goals I had in mind were to be as transparent as possible, expose the trend happening among our kids so that we might support each other, and, at the very least, we could all be aware and vigilant! Then I wanted to move on and privately handle my own household.

Even though I always offered proof of what I was claiming, the denial and fear was strong. Not one parent I contacted wanted to see that proof. Understandably, this was not a pleasant thing to hear. Personally, it made more sense to me to face this head on, but many people aren't willing or capable of being comfortably present with their fear, pain or shame. It triggered a lot of negative energy for them, while I was being transparent about my own. This was particularly the case if my own darkness shined a light on theirs. I found people would often get angry, quickly turn away or give harsh advice and opinions. Sometimes it was due to having the same painful issues hidden within their own family, but sometimes, it was coming from the belief that what we were going through was almost contagious.

Often it seems easier for others to blame us for the pain we are swimming in, as if it is somehow caused by something wrong with us and therefore is deserved. That seemed to be a reoccurring attitude. I felt the sense that people who knew of our struggle figured that if it was somehow caused or deserved by my family, maybe they were different and maybe their household was absolved, free and clear. Blaming Elliot, other family members, or me was a guarantee of immunity for *their* family. They were getting life right; we weren't; therefore, the monster wouldn't darken their door.

I eventually got used to the "friendly fire" and figured it was the nature of the beast and par for the course. It was deeply painful at first, but it then became nothing more than predictable and exasperating.

In the long run, no matter how hard we try to hide, deny or cover over the monsters in a family, the truth and misery of them become too much to bear or hide and things *must* be dealt with. Layer any family down and you will find areas that need work, focus and healing. It doesn't have to be a threat to discover those things—they are meant to be discovered. Things come out so they *can* be handled and healed. Hiding and denying because of shame, fear and whatever else makes the messy truth feel more threatening—stuffing it down and hiding it away—only keeps us unwell and in the dark.

Many times, just when I had exhausted my strategies, energy and sometimes my dignity, things would surprisingly calm down for a week or so, making me question the reality of the problem—*and* my sanity. Was it all even real? Or was I in an emotional frenzy and exaggerating the urgency? But before too long the old familiar telltale signs would appear. With tiny pin dot pupils, Elliot would be a little too excited and hyper in conversation. I nicknamed that behavior his "opiate chattering." Items and money would again go missing from home, and his addiction would present itself in various other ways.

When Elliot was actively on pills, his personality became condensed to only one of two moods: a very irritable, agitated, bad mood or an overly good, excited mood. No in-between. He would also randomly vomit and had constant sinus problems. Any those symptoms alone, let alone a combination of them, sent me into a panic, which resulted in angry confrontations and interrogations. It was a never-ending roller coaster.

One of those blow-ups resulted once again in Elliot spending a couple of months in my mom's spare bedroom, but inevitably, he wore out his welcome there with his mood swings or by hounding for her money and pills. He would then go to his dad's but would also wear out his welcome there, being caught in lies and deception. He would then circle around and return to me or go to a friend's house. He didn't stay any one place longer than a couple of months. This was a time of chaos and absolute misery. It was impossible to not get dragged into the fray if you were anywhere near our lives. A neutral corner was not realistic in such a dire situation.

When I would put Elliot out, my misery would take on different forms. When he was staying somewhere else, the fear of where he was and what he was experiencing, or who he might be at the mercy of . . . and even whether he would go to prison or die, took over and tormented me. Conflict surrounded him like a dust cloud. No matter who Elliot was around, an argument about his dad or me would soon follow. People were missiles to be used as weapons directed at us. It was exhausting and upsetting, I leaned heavily on my corner for support and dreaded conversations with anyone outside of it.

One afternoon when Elliot was staying with a friend, I came home from work to find a window had been forced open in a bedroom. I was horrified. I had a feeling it had been done by Elliot or someone related to me. When I got to the bottom of it, I found out my mother had helped Elliot get it open and climbed through it with him. They had retrieved clothing, a television set and other electronics. I had been holding onto these things to use as leverage to bargain with in my attempts to corner Elliot into going into treatment.

No words can describe my horror and anger when I found out that, not only had Elliot betrayed me and broken in, but my mother was now having to admit to doing it with him! I went hot and cold all over, feeling my pulse in various areas as my adrenaline surged. Not knowing what to do I called my police officer friend. He felt that a lesson needed to be taught. Since the situation had been going on for some time and seemed to be getting worse, and because my mother should be held accountable for so many things, he suggested I report them for breaking in.

I made the mistake of first calling my mom to let her know my things needed to be returned or I was going to file a police report. She had broken into her own daughter's home! It was against everything that was right—how in the world could she? It seemed the extreme opposite of how things should have been. I felt that I had no one. Those who I felt I should expect to support me, to side with me, or in the very least, to side with the truth and what was blatantly *right*, were behaving like my worst enemies. The stress and frustration were excruciating. My mother argued in circles that she had done nothing wrong and that it would be "unchristian" for me to get her in legal trouble.

We went 'round and 'round arguing who was right about what. I didn't feel strong enough to know how to handle it, so I decided to sleep on it. Over the next few days she gave a completely different version to several family members. Two of them called the pastors of my church to let them know, "*one of the church's members was false³ and was actually abusing and threating an elderly grandmother.*" Then my family members sent me copies of those emails to let me know I had "been exposed" to my church. I *burned* with humiliation. When would the nightmare end? How untrue and unfair could it possibly get? Church was one of my few safe places. All the while, Elliot's addiction was raging on, obstructed from view as conflict and insanity in the peripheral created the perfect distraction.

That was a buckle point for me. I climbed under the covers, closed the blinds and planned on staying there. I was surely never going to that church again! Much to my relief, one of the pastors from the church called to let me know not to worry; they were aware of my character and somewhat knew what I was going through. She said I was still safe to come to church without fear of being falsely accused or ganged up on because of whatever was going on in the family. I was assured I could safely trust in the kindness and support of my church family. Relief washed over me. Being validated and treated honorably, while being surrounded by people who were doing the opposite of what made sense, was so healing that it was almost painful.

That was one of the first times I felt released to pour out some of my family problems to anyone outside of my close circle or to those who already knew about my problems. Still fearing that I wouldn't be believed or that I would sound insane myself, I shared with her only limited amounts of what was going on with Elliot and what I had battled through thus far with a few family members (namely, my mother). As I shared my story, hot tears poured down my face and off my chin, but I was so accustomed to maintaining my composure that my voice remained calm. The kindness I received in that phone call was such a comfort for me, but the embarrassment resulting from that exposure to my church lasted for years. The scars within were stacking up on top of each other, blending with such confusion that I was soon unable to tell which pain or fear had been triggered when something sent me reeling into panic or a full blown meltdown.

Being new to the process of addiction treatment, and even though Elliot was still refusing, I endlessly researched treatment centers. I found one close to us that specialized in opiate problems. I was concerned that he would be there long enough—treatment time was less than a month. But it would be a start if he would just go. I saved the number in my phone so I could call as soon as we had a breakthrough. Things were so out of control that I feared I would receive news of his death before then. I began having dreams of him in a casket. Night and day I prayed he would become willing. Knowing he probably wasn't going to agree to go as he was active in addiction, I prayed that he would become so miserable in it that he would *become* willing.

Weeks went by with no communication, no news. Silence.

One day, when I was busy at work, Elliot called. I closed my office door and asked him where he was, how he was. He sounded feeble and sick. He asked if I would pick him up from my mother's house and take him somewhere so he could get sober. I didn't continue questioning him or bother to ask what prompted the call. I hung up, called a local treatment center, made the appointment for that afternoon to check him in, applied my insurance and wrote a check for the overage. I then raced to my mother's to pick him up.

The day turned into madness. No one was home at my mom's when I got there. I learned Elliot had her drive him to a seedy side of town to buy pills so he could dose up before checking in. I was livid. I later learned that it's common for someone heading to rehab, but at the time and in the stress of the moment, it sent me into a tailspin of fear and anger. Again, the fact that his grandmother participated in things that were so clearly wrong, was something I never calmed down about, but just resigning myself to getting him there and checked in, I said nothing. I waited and burned alive on the inside. I was used to the silent burn by then.

During the drive, Elliot was agitated and hateful. I ignored it and drove as fast as I could. When we got there, I was included in Elliot's check in, which took several hours. It was upsetting, exhausting and frustrating to say the least. But everything in life seemed to feel that way.

You often think it's going to be a situation of "once and done" the first time a substance abuser agrees to go away to get sober. My wish would be that were true for any family. And that was my hope when Elliot checked in. Filled with the enthusiasm to turn all of this around and have my son back, I jumped on board with Elliot's treatment, taking him creature comforts and gifts, and joining him for group classes and family therapy sessions. Elliot's mood swings during the first two weeks were outrageous. I took all of them personal, not understanding they were par for the course.

Oftentimes, when someone checks into treatment, they will begin to complain of conflict or discomfort. That is their addiction's way of wanting them to get out so they can return to using. I realized none of this so I fought hard to talk sense to him throughout it.

It was stressful beyond comprehension. You learn as you go.

At Christmas, Elliot was in treatment. I spent the holiday alone staring at the floor telling myself next Christmas would be amazing, I just had to get through this *one*. I felt weak from blinking back tears all day and forcing myself to be strong and positive. It was a terrible, terrible time. I should have just let it all release instead of denying myself the right to feel terrible, but you learn as you go.

The day after Christmas, I drove to the treatment center for Elliot's scheduled family counseling session. The counselor, one I had not met with prior, was waiting for me when I arrived. She was very abrupt when she buzzed me in and turned her back to me, walking ahead through the double doors to the meeting room. She was heavyset, much older than most of the staff and had an air about her—like she was an angry school teacher. I sensed that I was in trouble and being escorted to the principal's office. My energy contracted, and I wasn't sure why, but I felt completely on guard. Elliot was sitting alone when we got to the room; she sat down beside him and rubbed his hand. I cringed. The session opened with a discussion of hyper-strict, abusive parenting. My heart sank, I knew exactly what was going to happen without having to sit and stomach it. She gently told my son, "It's all right, baby, you're safe." ("Baby"? She called him . . . baby?)

I tried to speak up but knew I had to do it calmly. I was so well-trained in being made to look wrong and awful because of experiences with my mother, that I knew any angry or defensive reaction would make lies seem true. "Elliot . . ." I said as calmly as possible, "Please tell her we don't have a break down in our relationship and that our problems are an addiction issue. Please tell her the truth. Come on, don't do this here." Elliot looked at the floor. I turned to the counselor, with humility and respect and said, "Ma'am, my son is given expectations and consequences, but he is not mistreated. He is no stranger to love and appropriate affection. I promise you. If you are believing otherwise, there is manipulation going on here."

I turned to Elliot hoping he would validate the truth based on sheer conscience. He was expressionless. She was nothing like any of the counselors we had worked with there so far, who didn't seem easily manipulated or at all eager to assign blame . . . let alone false blame! She cut me off and took over for the remainder of the hour. I sat silently and took it. Saying nothing, as Elliot blamed his addiction on a lack of love and understanding. On coldness and unreasonable criticism. I burned with frustration but I knew it was futile to defend the truth any further. Clearly it didn't matter.

When we left the session room I turned to him and said nothing, but fire blazed in my eyes. Elliot could see I was furious. He spoke first. "Did you like that?" he asked with half a grin and a nod. "Did you like how she believed me instead of you? She believed the *addict*. Isn't that awesome? When you're the one she should have believed! Did you like that? Did you?" He walked off down the hall smiling back at me over his should like a cat with a canary.

That moment I was caught cold, absolutely unprepared for how deceptive my own child could be. I practiced a breathing technique to keep from vomiting. My legs were shaking as I walked back to my car, defeated. I drove home feeling completely hopeless. I didn't reach out to Elliot for a few days after that. When I finally did call to check on him, we both acted like it hadn't even happened. I didn't know where to begin anyway.

For the remaining days in treatment Elliot seemed to improve and even took accountability for some of his behaviors in the past. He enthusiastically told me that his plan was to get out, continue meeting with a sponsor, go to meetings and stay sober.

The day Elliot came home he relapsed. He convinced me he had to go to a meeting alone but was meeting several other people there who were also trying to stay sober. I allowed him to take his truck that I had been withholding and go alone. He didn't go to a meeting; instead, he went out with friends he had met in treatment, which is often not a healthy bond. They bought painkillers illegally and went to a party. I discovered the truth in his text messages.

square one. I felt like life would never get better and the /ay this would come to an end was with my son a cell or a cas... .t.

I told Elliot to pack his things and find a place to stay because, unless he was going to work a program with honesty, he could not remain with me. I sat in the rocking chair my father bought me to rock Elliot in when he was an infant and watched as he feverishly gathered his things in a trash bag and walked out the door. I had no idea where he was headed nor did I know where or how he would end up. My grief was brutal. I had never felt so sad and alone in my life. I sat in that chair for hours, remembering how he smelled so clean as a baby. Remembering when he learned to crawl, walk, read. I thought of his first day in Kindergarten, how we followed him with a camera all the way in. I could almost smell the classroom and hear the sounds from that day. I thought of his face, his clothes, his activities at every age. Like a movie the years poured through my heart as I rocked myself in that chair feeling as though the world was falling from under me. My heart was in a million pieces. I was beginning to think his addiction would kill us both.

Annie's Message: Doing the right things, doing the hard but crucial things for the greater good of the situation will often feel absolutely horrendous.

ROUND SEVEN

Unrelenting Heartache

You become a champion by fighting one more round. When things are tough you fight one more round. —Gentleman Jim Corbett

Turmoil: A state of great disturbance, confusion or uncertainty.[1]

PASSING ELLIOT BACK AND FORTH, putting him out, having him end up at a different friend or family member's house or who knows where . . . had become my way of life. Life was so chaotic and miserable on a daily basis that I didn't know what to do when I had a quiet evening. Except worry or catch up on tears I held in. I was used to the adrenaline surging inside me, it was common to be sick to my stomach and in fight or flight mode at all times.

The Elliot I'd raised, who had any ability to be reasoned with, seemed to have disappeared; his evil twin was in control.

I wasted a lot of time trying to figure out what caused Elliot's addiction. Was it because of the family I came from? Could it be one of the many challenges or traumatic situations we had been through? Was it genetics? Was I too strict? Too inexperienced as a mother? Or maybe it was caused by imperfections from his Dad's side? Did family divorces contribute? I analyzed up one side and down the other, mentally combing through behaviors I'd seen, known mistakes, and flaws. It could be many things!

When addiction rises up in your family, at first you tend to pass the blame around like a bad cold. Elliot jumped right on board with those notions. He would argue every point viciously like a seasoned prosecuting attorney. Elliot learned to use anyone and anything he could put the blame on to either gather sympathy and gain something or to distract from what he was up to. He would use anything; nothing was sacred no matter how ridiculous. He would make a sharp, painful point to get what he was after or deflect from truth and accountability.

Addicts are great at arguing! They will go fishing for your sympathy as a bargaining tool to get you to take them in, give them money or help them out however they need it. If that doesn't work in the moment, they sometimes switch to shame and guilt, reminding you what they'd been through in life and in what areas you are a failure.

That is one of the worst parts of the madness! I had to train myself not to get sucked into it nor to make decisions because of it. Getting pulled in was when the worst manipulations occurred.

We were a mess!

∽

Suffering has been stronger than all other teaching and has taught me to understand what your heart used to be. I have been bent and broken, but . . . I hope . . . into a better shape.
— Charles Dickens

My participation in the madness was making me as crazy as the madness itself. I was constantly hunting for information, snooping through everything, driving by where he might be, and researching to find out everything I could about anyone he was involved with. I analyzed my behaviors and motives like I did his. I wondered if maybe I was running myself ragged in order to make *myself* feel safe about his safety. Whatever the case may be, nothing I was doing was working. I wasn't bringing it to an end; I wasn't helping; and truthfully, none of it was doing any good. I knew what I needed to know, my son was horribly dependent on pain medication and it was stealing his life and swallowing his soul. Because of it, he was in danger and couldn't be trusted. He was spending time around frightening people who were also addicted and he was exposed to terrible things and places. He needed to decide for himself that he wanted a better life. Those were the facts. Nothing more for me to find out and there was nothing more I could do.

I was fighting for Elliot's life more than he was; in fact, I was starting to realize that I was fighting for Elliot's life *against* him.

At some point you come to realize you can no more prevent your child's death by overdose or any other drug related situation than you can from a car accident or cancer. I could do everything possible to not make it easy for him, but I couldn't pull him out of it. The nightmare was devouring both of us.

Adding to the madness and heartache, my mother continued to make things worse in the name of doing what she thought was best. She was a "passenger issue" that aggravated every crucial matter and just about cost me my mind. I really needed support. I would grieve for the mother I never had during the worst moments of Elliot's out-of-control addiction. No attempt to get through to her worked: letters, calls, mean arguments, tearful pleading, having others try to speak with her. Nothing. It was useless to try. His addiction continued and her part in it only got worse. She continued to argue steadfastly for his needs, to take his side and to cause more problems. Sporadically, she would call to plead with one of us to help him, to come get him or to help her with him because he was exhausting her—but then she would interfere with our efforts, standing between Elliot and consequences. She would not listen to the professionals who consistently gave her one solution: "*Stay out of it.*"

We cycled through deeper and darker over and again.

And then just like that, of the blue, Elliot shaped up for a few weeks and held it together long enough to come back home but under tight watch. It didn't take long not to feel at ease. There was a hate coming from him just below the surface. It seemed to rise from him in vapors, like steam. It made me sad, missing my happy son, and it was also a fearful thing as I could sense a dangerous difference in him. He was easily triggered. I realized later that his explosions were mostly fueled by withdrawal and opiate cravings. Every argument or frustration took him straight to level ten, red line anger. I knew he couldn't last for long in my home again.

I required Elliot go to church with me on Sundays as long as he was staying in my home. One particular morning, as he was getting ready, I noticed he was paying extra careful attention to a duffel bag in his bedroom. I decided I needed to figure out a way to search through it. Driving to church as usual, I devised a reason to stop by my mother's after. My plan was to speed off when Elliot went inside for whatever it was I made up for him to ask for, something such as eggs, sugar, or some other quick, random necessity. As church was ending, there was a tension between us. I was extra paranoid knowing what I was about to do and how far into chaos it could take us. Things tend to escalate very quickly when you have desperate, volatile addicts in your life.

I told Elliot I needed to stop and have him run into his grandmother's. Pulling into the driveway as planned, he seemed to suspect nothing. As he was walking in, I quickly stepped on the gas and drove off. I saw in the rear view that Elliot had jumped off her porch, over the railing and was racing around her car. My mother was not far behind him with the keys! I couldn't believe it. He must have yelled for her to grab them and hurry. The race was on to my house! I knew she would side with Elliot, do whatever he said and ask questions later. *So unfair!* I thought. I was fuming.

I pulled up to the garage and was preparing to run inside and search Elliot's bag as fast as I could get my hands on it, but I wasn't quick enough. My mother's car came squealing around the corner. Elliot jumped out, threw a water bottle over my head breaking a window and charged past me into the house. My mother was shaking her fist at me, shouting for me to stop acting crazy and leave Elliot alone. It was unbelievable. Why in the world would she side with a known addict, even if he was her grandson? She was well aware of his problems and my desperation for him to recover. I was his mother! And I was *her daughter*, it was all so twisted. I felt Elliot would never be free with her in the picture! I stood there dazed, my hands and feet went cold. We hadn't had a great history, but this was clearly and obviously wrong. How in the world could she side against her own child? Her child who was probably not in the wrong? She knew the consequences of his addiction could lead to his death and that was the cause for my fight. I just couldn't process it. I felt hated and I felt hate for her rise in return within me like bile.

My motive for everything was to protect the health and life of my son! My mother's participation caused a constant monsoon of emotions to rage within me. I thought that she might just be what prevents my son from ever coming to reality and having a normal life. The confusion and rage I felt were engulfing, considering the parenting she had *not* given me, coupled with having to endure all of her interfering and harassing, as I became a mother myself. I couldn't believe the warped irony. Those things were hard enough to move beyond peacefully. In my perspective, she had now crossed over and become my enemy. The lines were drawn. I realized one of the biggest battles I'd face might be going standing toe-to-toe with members of my family, most notably my own mother.

My grief over not having a mother, especially when I needed one the most, had to take a backseat to what was most important—Elliot making it out of this alive.

Elliot came back out of the house and walked past me with clothes in his arms and the duffel bag over his shoulder, apparently planning to sleepover at his grandmother's. We didn't speak as he breezed past, and my mother and I glared at each other. This had to stop; she had to be stopped; it *had to come to an end*, somehow. I felt like I was watching my son commit suicide with my arms tied behind my back—and with my mother present and helping! The heartache was relentless. She could not hear that she was wickedly in the wrong, she couldn't even hear that it wasn't her place to be involved. It was painful. My fear was that my mother would enable my son all the way to a prison cell or a casket. I watched him drive off with her with my mouth open and my hands in the air. When I walked inside, I felt as if I weighed a thousand pounds and yet, I felt weightless. Nothing was real.

Once inside, I dropped to my knees, buried my face in the couch and screamed until my throat was raw and I thought I'd pass out. And then I stood up and tried to feel human. I had no idea what to do or what might possibly happen next. One person at a time, I called my close circle of support to give them the newest unbelievable update. Looking at the battle as a boxer, I thought of each one of them as though they played a role as my corner-men. My therapist and police officer friends served as my chief seconds, faithful as always in my corner giving me direction and strategy. My coworker and two best friends who let me scream, shout, analyze and rant on and on endlessly were faithful cut-men, carefully tending to my wounds and injuries. I needed them desperately.

Those conversations were the only thing to soothe me—to a point. But the nightmare and my heart raced on.

Exhausted, I sat down on my floor and wrote out all that had happened. I poured out all the pain that was in my heart into a journal. I then jotted down what my basic needs and strategies would be. I had to find a way of forcing myself to stop dwelling on the past. I couldn't keep thinking of who my child *used* to be. I knew I also needed to force myself to stop dwelling on the future and who I was hoping he would become, versus how he might very well end up. As sad or terrifying as it all might be, I had control over none of it. I decided to focus only on what I could do that day. I had no choice, I needed a break.

Elliot wasn't with my mother long; soon he went to stay with his dad again. While he was there, my mother stayed in constant, secret contact with him even though I had made it clear she was to remain out of the picture. Her involvement caused unending arguments and problems between us. Again, I realized there was not much more I could do about any of it. Living in constant conflict and turmoil was killing me as much as it was a huge distraction from focusing on solving the real and pressing issues. In those months, I avoided contact with my mother or anyone involved with her; I focused on work and calming my mind down. I had enough to process and cope with without exhausting myself with discord that never ended.

When things were calm, I grieved for the presence and personality of Elliot. Even though he was no longer a minor, he was still very young. I hadn't let go of the mindset that he should be with me and be cared for under my watch. That would come much later. I felt a combination of an empty nest along with the aftershocks of terror and pain from living in a crisis.

When you can't have your child live with you because doing so creates an unpeaceful environment, it's very hard and you miss them *terribly*. Life felt so unfair.

Annie's Message: The demon of addiction is something I could never figure out. There is no logic to it. It doesn't have a head or a tail; it just is—and it is with a vengeance. It reminds me of the movie Predator. Just when you think the danger has passed, it takes on a new form and comes back even more viciously. Addiction is a family crisis; it is not isolated to the addict themselves nor to the one or two people closest to it—it's a monster that can devour the whole family. Addiction exposes dysfunction in every person connected to it. Just as the addict must recover and heal, so must each family member. Addiction takes you places you never thought you would go and causes you to do things you never thought you would do.

ROUND EIGHT

Hope Rises & Falls

A champion is someone who gets up when he can't.
—Jack Dempsey

Uncertainty: Something that is doubtful or unknown.[1] Unpredictable, unreliable, risky.

DURING THE MONTHS Elliot spent living with his dad, life began to feel as though a level of peace and regularity returned. I felt there was hope for the future again. I hated that Elliot was an hour's drive away from me, but we visited regularly, talked on the phone daily and seemed to be healing enough to resume our old, jovial, loving relationship. I even started spending some of my time socially, something I hadn't felt comfortable doing much of in the past.

When you carry the burden of a child in trouble, it is all you can do to hold the dam back when asked about them by someone outside your safety circle. To hear how anyone else's family is doing can also be overwhelming. Having dealt with so much shame, dysfunction, fear and anxiety my whole life, I wasn't one to run in social settings for long anyway. But I felt relaxed enough to get out here and there. I could actually laugh without feeling tense. I didn't have a sense of foreboding that bad news could be lurking and the other shoe might drop at any time.

Unfortunately, it was short lived!

I had always been highly sensitive to patterns of behavior, my son's especially. Having been raised in an environment where in order to feel safe I had to be on guard and hyper-aware, I never lost my extreme sensitivity to energy and patterns of behavior. I had a strong sense of what was just under the surface, beyond what was being said or done. For instance, if Elliot would complain too excessively about a particular person or a conflict, I knew that was against his carefree, easygoing personality and meant something beyond the surface was going on. I also caught on to the fact that when he was being accused of something and ranted about it more than a few times, the probability was that he had actually done it. My intuition panned out often enough that I trusted it.

When you have an addict in your life, you have to look at all possibilities of reality and truth, otherwise you will be easily fooled and horribly disappointed time and again. To my few select and trusted confidants, I began to describe Elliot as a "unique addict." My description was, "Elliot will steal your purse and help you look for it."

Even when desperately addicted, Elliot was charming, friendly and noticeably well-mannered. He has always had a way of getting on your exact level. I often said, "My son doesn't come across as though he's trying to sell you something or charm you—you don't know you're being charmed. Elliot doesn't convince you he's awesome, he convinces you that *you're* awesome." People always loved him for that. But when he was deep in the throes his addiction and operating as "the evil twin," he would use that charm and charisma in a selfish and evil way. That is when he could do a world of damage. He would more than break my heart—he would turn my whole world upside down and make me question everything I ever believed in.

Elliot returned from his dad's to our hometown about eight months later, but within a matter of months he was back to the same old addiction and its pathology. My heart returned to my shoes and my thought was "here we go again." He returned directly to the madness of his addiction—rushing back in with all of the old patterns, situations and scary individuals. Surely my heart should have gotten used to falling through my knees by now.

We were in the repeat cycle: Elliot would come home and would be the model son—until he wasn't! So once again he packed his things and made the usual trek from my home to grandma's. I despised when he was there as much as I did when he stayed at the home of a stranger. She fed his addiction and addict behavior. It didn't really matter if he was there or on the street, he was really not much safer. However, it didn't take long this time before too many problems arose from his behavior in her home that she told him to leave (in her car) and not come back until he got control. He ended up sleeping in her car in a grocery store parking lot even though it was the dead of winter and he was sick with a throat and ear infection.

I felt ruthless as a mother to see this, but there was no way I could take him in. This addiction would kill him if he didn't get into a program. Not only did he need to get medical care, but he also needed to separate from the storms he was causing. Elliot brought chaos, crisis and criminal types of people around. In his addiction, he became unbearable and destructive in any setting. I felt that he simply had to go to treatment again and get clean permanently, no other option!

~

A smooth sea never made a skillful sailor.
–Franklin D. Roosevelt

I showed up to that grocery store and leaned into the car several times a day to check on him. Each time I would ask if he was ready to throw in the towel, but he would not agree to my terms of going to rehab. I offered to take him there—I would even pay for it— but I would take him nowhere else. Bottom line: he would have to remain out on his own like this, living in a car with nothing and no one unless he agreed. The addiction was ravaging him. He was skin and bones and had a defeated look in his eyes that transcended being cold and sick. For days we were in a standoff and he would not budge. He would start the car to keep warm or go visit someone for a few hours and then return to that parking lot and sleep, buried under a mountain of blankets. I continued to show up every few hours and remind him of baseball games, vacations, holidays and cookouts. I mentioned clean, warm showers, lunch dates . . . anything normal I could think of! I would then ask him if this is how he imagined ending up. I asked if he felt that was an awesome way to live. Each time he would stubbornly stare at the steering wheel and say, "I'm doing fine."

I wanted him to think his answers through as he said them; I wanted him to realize his true conditions—something had to click!

Nothing.

Then I would leave, telling him before I left that I loved him more than anything and anyone in this world and that I would drop everything to get him into treatment the second he said the word. After that, I would drive away, my heart hemorrhaging and tears rolling down my face. I would call my support circle and ask, "When does it end? What is his threshold?" No one had answers and no one could console my agony or change the circumstances. The pain warred against me. When you experience long-term stress, you kind of lose yourself—at least I started to and it wasn't fun. I lost control often and sometimes felt I would lose my mind.

I wouldn't act out so much as I would sometimes leave work and lie in bed weeping for hours. I would hunt for information or drive by different homes expecting to see Elliot there. It didn't help! Oftentimes, I would not remember stretches of road I had driven and would suddenly realize I had missed my exit. When a conflict arose with Elliot or a situation felt unbearable, I would drop to my knees screaming and crying for hours. Most of the time I couldn't talk about it without ending up shouting. Thoughts of Elliot consumed me.

One day, a friend was coming over to visit me for lunch, and just before she was due to arrive, I discovered a message from Elliot asking someone if he had any pills available. I thought, *but we've just had a few good weeks!* By the time my friend arrived, I was a mess. I answered my door wearing sunglasses and told her I couldn't face anyone for the rest of the day. She was very kind and understanding and asked if she could come in for just a few minutes to be a comfort to me. We sat on the couch in silence for a long time. She kept saying "I can't do anything, but I am here." I never took the sunglasses off during her entire visit.

Once I zoned out at a traffic light until the lady in the car behind me laid on her horn. She pulled around beside me to pass and I gave her the middle finger with one hand and made a pig nose at her with the other, yelling, "Stop hogging the road!" Judging by the look on her face, she was stunned. I put my head on the steering wheel and asked myself, *What are you DOING?*

When cortisol and adrenaline would hit me, I'd find myself surging with panic or anger in a full-blown "fight or flight" response. It was like an out of body experience!

When I wasn't at home, I would be tempted to go find him and bring him home to me. I would imagine him again in pajamas as a little boy, smelling like he had just taken a bath, smiling and running through the house. Before I was too tempted to end the standoff and bring the cycle back into my home, I would pull out the note I kept in my purse of a hand drawn casket with his name on it. I penciled in his date of birth and always updated his date of death to a month or so in the future—my personal reminder that if I kept him comfortable in his addiction, death is where he would likely end up. Time seemed to move slowly through those days. I couldn't sleep or eat, and at work I stared at clients and my computer like a zombie, pretending to function while wondering how many times I could possibly sink into this heartache and misery. I hated life. I resented anyone who seemed to have it perfect. Or normal. Or easy.

I figured I'd wait Elliot out through his days in the car. Standing firm, feinting the strength of my resolve, hoping desperately that he would cave in. I thought surely he'd soon become miserable enough to agree to check into a treatment center. I'd found another one out of state and was ready and waiting to make that trip, but as usual, my hopes were sky high! But after three or four days in the car, a well-meaning friend took him in. Elliot was in that home for a few months and shattered his relationships there as well, but not before I called and left messages for the parent living there. She refused to hear me every time I tried to give her the warning that Elliot was abusing pills and who knows what else, along with her son, who appeared to be in as bad shape as Elliot. But Elliot got to her first. Bitter conflicts ensued. She made it clear Elliot's dad and I were not welcome to give her any information about our child nor any advice. I burned alive inside.

Elliot's dad and I spent hours on the phone outraged and wracking our brains about what to do. By all appearances, Elliot was on the brink of death in one way or another. I sent an email to the mother letting her know she was hindering my son's decision to agree to treatment and live. I told her that if he overdosed and died during his stay in her home, I'd be on her porch with nothing to lose. Madness all over again! She responded, telling me she saw nothing wrong with Elliot. He was kind and well-mannered and she was happy to have him. She told his father and I that we should feel shame for turning our son away and accusing him of being an addict when he clearly was not. I could not believe this could be happening again in yet another household!

Another flash knockdown. I was an expert at shaking those off and getting back up right away. But I was growing weary. Another household filled with new opponents and whatever personality types were added to the fight. Would it ever end? The number of opponents seemed to grow consistently. If it wasn't new adversaries, it was the discovery that those I thought would be supportive and against the drug abuse soon proved to be on the opposing side.

Elliot was like a hot potato at this point—no one could hold on to him for long. He and that parent soon had a falling out and he was back on his own. I went weeks at a time having no idea where he was. When he called his voice sounded rough. Even his way of speaking sounded different. He was using more slang and swearing freely, something he had been too respectful to do around me or any other adult. My heart was breaking. My son was disappearing.

Going through the routines of mundane life is not an easy thing when you have long-term misery and fear hovering over your heart. It was incredibly hard to focus, almost impossible. I was always distracted, forgetful and clumsy. I was on edge and easily upset. I stayed close to home, leaving only for work, church and necessary errands. Keeping my world small, I waited to see what would unfold, walking the floors at night in prayer for my son's life, health and future. My heart felt like it was full of hot stones and my stomach full of bitter acid. Elliot never left my thoughts, no matter where I was or what I was doing. I cared about nothing else.

Out walking my dog one afternoon, I was stopped by a group of kids I recognized from Elliot's high school years. They asked how he was doing, and as always, I had little to say. One of them asked me if I knew about Elliot paying a drug dealer with fake board game money. No, I hadn't. In an animated manner, they went on to tell me how Elliot knew the lighting was dark in this particular house so he'd given a one hundred-dollar bill from a board game to a dealer in exchange for pills, then hurried out. It caused a fight after he left; the friends who remained took the punches for him. One of the kids shrugged as he chimed in "The thing about Elliot, though, is we all liked him too much to stay mad." Those guys loved him too, as shady as they were. They preferred someone else take his beating for him anyway. Justice was still served. No one stayed mad. We all have love for Elliot.

The situation pretty well summed up life.

*Annie's Message: I couldn't understand why each time the cycle was greater than the last. Later I learned it's because addiction is chronic **and progressive.***

ROUND NINE

Hands Off, Gloves Off

Everyone has a plan until they get punched in the face.
—Mike Tyson

Detach: To disengage, unfasten, disconnect,[1] unhook, free. To separate from something or send on a different mission.
Surrender: to agree to stop fighting, hiding, resisting, etc., because you know that you will not win or succeed.[2]

WEEKS TURNED INTO MONTHS with no real or lasting relief. I felt as if I was losing my ability to carry the stress and function normally. I walked around with a monster on my back, not letting on to anyone outside my close circle that I felt like I was dying inside. Small aggravations would send me through the roof—a cashier being rude, a mistake in my checking account. Things like that absolutely did me in. I could carry the crisis itself, but I couldn't handle small upsets poking at me as I carried the weight of it. It was too much.

Elliot and I were at constant odds at this point. I still desperately wanted him to go to a treatment facility. Anything to pull him out of the death trap. He was stubborn in his refusing. He continued to bounce from family, to friends to strangers' homes until, when finally when he'd worn out every welcome, he slept in a dugout at the baseball park where he grew up hitting home runs and grand slams over the fence.

By now, Elliot weighed less than I did, I could see the outline of his teeth through his cheeks. His clothes hung on him. He was a barely shadow of the animated, bulky athlete that my heart clung to a picture of. It was like seeing a hijacked version of my child. I wasn't sure how much longer he had. It was devastating. For a mother, it feels like death by a thousand cuts—at least for me it did. I felt like getting into bed and giving up. But I knew I couldn't; I had to endure. As long as he was living, I would cling to hope.

One thing I knew with total certainty: I couldn't give Elliot comfort in the pit he was in. I had to force him to hate it and bear it. I had hope that he would become miserable enough to hate his life as much as I did and decide his way out of it. For whatever need he had, except for surrendering to treatment, my back was turned. That was the fight. As a mother who wanted to rush in with comfort and loyalty to their child, that fight felt like death. But I realized *it's the only way he would make it out.*

I began noticing the path my thoughts would take. If I opened my ear to anything or anyone negative, it adversely effected my hope and belief for the outcome. I would go down a dark hole of worry and despair. If I browsed through upsetting or meaningless social media, I would sense myself losing heart. My mind would flood with one possible tragedy after another, and before too long, I was expecting something terrible and reacting to everything as if disaster was imminent that very day! On the flip side, if I practiced peace and believed in the best outcome, if I walked my mind through the best case scenario, I believed in that, and my energy would be boosted by it. When I would call a confidant and say, "I can't do this!" and get the response, "Yes you can! You're *doing* it," I would believe it and fight just a little longer.

I learned to tell myself that even though the current circumstances were terrible, it didn't mean my faith wasn't working. It meant the current circumstances . . . were terrible! Faith is *fortified* by believing despite the terrible, by believing through to the other side and seeing the triumph. I told myself I would believe against all evidence to the contrary. I was going to believe that everything was working out in our favor! Until and unless it didn't, I would believe it was going to happen.

You gather evidence to support your theories in life, and my faith was extremely sensitive to negative predictions. I couldn't hear from anyone suggesting something tragic would befall my son. It wasn't happening that day! Therefore, even if it was a possibility, I couldn't hear about it unless I had to face it. I was going to bear down and believe for the exact opposite to happen. I needed to gather evidence that what I was believing in would come about. My son would *live* and not die; he would choose his way upward, forward, onward, and we would have a great life! "It's going to work out even better than I expect!" became my mantra against every disturbance.

I analyzed my fears and how they drove me. It dawned on me that some of my outrageous, over-the-top efforts weren't totally about doing what was *best* for my son, or even the greater good of us all. Some of the crazy things I would do to try to drag him out of the addiction seemed to be more about *my* need to feel Elliot was safe. I had become a mauler-type fighter and that was smothering my life more than it was helping my son's. My efforts were not causing him to be safe nor even care if he was. Of course I wanted him to be safe and healthy. I cared about his safety more than anything, but my fears were obsessive, unhealthy and not at all effective! I was driving a car that was long out of gas. I had to ask myself, was I really doing the right things? Was all the night and day ruminating, dwelling, researching, analyzing, plotting . . . was it even doing anything? He was still dangerously addicted and getting worse. Was I chasing after him, terrorized and driven by the fear of the pain that losing him would cause? It seemed as if my pursuit was nothing more than a frenzied race in a hamster wheel.

Maybe I was only delaying the process for Elliot. Maybe I needed to give up fighting and somehow surrender him. I decided that for a while I needed to figure out how to calm and heal my own life instead of racing along with his.

～

Whatever it is you're seeking won't come in the form you're expecting. —Haruki Murakami

I thought back to a time when I had to let go of my fears and let him figure it out. When Elliot was around eight years old, my sister and I took him roller skating one afternoon at a skating rink. After we had been there about an hour a line formed for a Limbo contest. All of the kids lining up were bigger and older than Elliot, mostly in their early teens. Elliot skated over to me with the biggest smile on his face and said he was going to get in line. Without hesitating, I raised my hand up and said, "No, no, you can't do that, they're all older than you!" Fear had risen to the surface from deep within. Fear of my son being rejected, embarrassed and of losing. Whatever the case may be, I was afraid of it for him! He had been through so much already, and I thought I couldn't bear seeing him endure anymore heartache. My sister turned to me and said, "Let him go for it! Don't put what you might be afraid of on *him*. We have always had to live with fears, but look at him, he isn't afraid and that's awesome! Don't put fear into him!"

Realizing how right she was I nodded for h'
I watched from the side of the rink as Ellio'
circles with all of those kids, and wouldn't yo
that contest! The look on his face when he came ɪ..._ _
me, holding the First Place Ribbon, was something I will always
remember.

Sometimes things work out better than we would ever expect
when we let go of our fears and our fear-based effort to control
situations. Most of our fears come from our own needs and
experiences more than what is actually best in the present situation.

That day at the skating rink taught me a lifelong lesson that I
would need to return to many times, especially when it came to
how to handle my responses to Elliot's life. I knew I was facing one
of those times again. It was way past time to take my hands off and
let Elliot go and figure it out for himself.

I had hit the wall with Elliot's addiction. I realized I was
absolutely outmatched and powerless. My résumé, or lack thereof,
didn't matter; my parenting accomplishments or failures did not
matter. Nothing I could do, say, think or attempt made a lasting
difference. Anytime I had been disappointed by the dead-end of
my efforts, it was because I had mistaken ideas about dysfunction
and addiction.

I believe it all comes back to beliefs and the truth. I lifted my
hands and fell upon the source of my faith to take over. I started
to wonder if maybe wherever my son was might be right where he
needed to be in order for his journey to unfold exactly as it was
supposed to. I was in the way.

Elliot's journey might not play out and look like I expected. It
might not unfold in the way I was trying to get it to unfold—but,
maybe that was okay. I needed to give it space; I needed to breathe;
and I needed trust that things would work out. I no longer felt that

vas my place to be a contender in Elliot's fight.
That was the hardest thing ever!

~

Expectation is the root of all heartache.
—William Shakespeare

It was time to take off the gloves and lay it all down. The struggle was over for me. It was time to lean on my faith, to carry my heart and my son to safety.

I intentionally went out of town during those days Elliot was sleeping in the dugout. I couldn't stand to be around for it. One of the hardest phases in life for me is always the "until"—when I'm between an experience and the outcome. In the middle of effort and result. That space in time. It's silent and it's loud. The "in-between" and "until" span of time is where everything in me works its way to the surface. It's when any bad habit, any negative characteristic, rises to the top. If I am triggered to panic, it's loud and it's explosive. If I'm on edge and sensitive, it's to the extreme.

But in the silent space—the baking, boiling, refiner's fire process—where things are just about to fall into place, or completely fall apart, I had to consciously set intentions. In this space, like during a pregnancy, I stepped up healthy behaviors and my integrity. I kept myself as calm as possible. I put in positive effort, but not with frenzied and controlling energy hoping to direct everyone's course just because I'm in panic. Instead, it had to be a calm space.

I put myself there in that silent space. And with that decision I gave Elliot the "gift of desperation."

Only a couple days later, Elliot *finally* realized and admitted to himself that he hated his current life and so he surrendered. On his own, Elliot booked a flight for himself from Ohio to California to go into what would be his second treatment center. It was our long awaited breakthrough—Elliot did it for himself.

A friend from my small circle of confidants drove him to the airport. Her brother had recently passed away from an overdose of medication after a car accident. She had Elliot hold his obituary and read it over and over on the way to the airport. This phase of battling the heavyweight contender of addiction had ended. It happened with an intervention from a higher power and a decision made by Elliot. My gloves were off. Elliot would have to fight for himself this time. Elliot finally stepped into the fight.

Annie's Message: As long as there's breath, there's hope. The greater the battle, the greater the victory.

ROUND TEN

Life Calms Down – Or So I Thought

Getting hit motivates me. It makes me punish the guy more. A
fighter takes a punch, hits back with three punches.
—Roberto Duran

Relapse: A reoccurrence of symptoms of a disease after a period of improvement.[1]
Renovate: To make changes and repairs so that it is back in good condition,[2] to make new or as if new again. To rebuild.
Restore: To bring back into existence,[3] to reestablish law and order.[4] To clean, repair, bring, or put back into original or better condition. To give back.

ONCE ELLIOT HAD BEEN IN CALIFORNIA for a few months, he suffered a setback—a relapse. I was pretty crushed having thought we had come through it permanently. Little did I know.

October, 2013: I was in a panic. Here Elliot was 2,300 miles across the country in yet another drug rehab facility for a painkiller addiction and I couldn't get ahold of him. As it turned out, he had charmed a staff member at this treatment center into giving him some extra freedom and skipping drug tests. She even gave him *money* for "clothes." Once again, a professional trained in addiction and manipulation, was manipulated by my polite, friendly, charming, drug-addicted son. That's my Elliot! He still had a haymaker in him to throw in the ring.

Obviously after the five years we had just experienced and two treatment centers, I'd lost faith in rehab centers, let alone a luxurious one that overlooked the beautiful beaches of Southern California. It didn't feel like true consequences to me and Elliot had put us through a lot. Even after he left our hometown, I figured it was a matter of time before he'd get himself in trouble and be back in Ohio, headed for death or prison. My heart was afraid to relax. Elliot had been an expert at bouncing from church, to relative, to treatment as proof he was conquering his issue . . . only to return to us worse each time. I was extremely skeptical and didn't have hope that anyone would know how to handle him, especially not someone unfamiliar with his patterns and pathology. His personality had won favor over truth too many times. This latest attempt at getting his life together felt as temporary as the rest.

~

Wherever you go . . . there you are. —Confuscious

I aggressively tried to track Elliot down, making calls and threatening some of the staff of this treatment center (I was still capable of being triggered back to my crazy).

I was beginning to lose hope when the Director of SOBA Recovery Center, Greg Hannley, called to tell me that Elliot was going to be transferred from the second treatment center to SOBA. (Ironically, Greg Hannley was a former boxing manager.)

I explained Elliot's personality and our experiences to Greg— specifically how easily Elliot fooled most people. I stressed how even school teachers had sided with him and explained that once a police officer had come to me after a drug-fueled argument saying,

"I'm not sure what is going on here Ma'am, but you have a great kid who says *you* are the addict. I hope you work your life out." The truth never seemed to have a chance, let alone a permanent solution.

After listening to me rant about our life for over an hour, Greg said, "Ohhh okay. So, basically Elliot is an amazing, good-looking, athletic, clean-cut kid with a great personality, excellent manners and tons of talent . . . but we can believe nothing he says?"

I was silent for a moment, always afraid of not being believed. "Yeah, pretty much." I told him.

"Okay yep, I've got sixty kids just like him here; he's in the right place." Those words allowed me to breathe.

That October day was the first time I believed my son would live to see twenty-three years old. That day marked the true end of my own personal uphill, tactical battle against my son to save his own life.

Elliot had a second setback after this one, but was on his own to come forward and ask for help out of it. I was no longer trying to be the rails to guide him in any direction. I realized, no matter where he went, his issues were more internal than externally manageable. Elliot took his misery with him. He had carried the dysfunction and desire with him across the country where he knew no one.

People will tell you that you have to get addicts out of their environment, but that is not always the answer. My son was across the nation, yet still managed to get his hands on substances. Desire can indeed trump geography. Wherever you go, there you are.

On his own, Elliot worked it out; he worked it through, and he is daily working a program.

Today Elliot is sober; he is trustworthy; he is sane and he is alive. He now coaches and plays on a softball team in Malibu—not bad for the "typical strung-out addict" who lived for a time in a dugout.

No matter how desperate and dark it got, no matter how hopeless it looked, I refused to give up or enable my son to be a drug addict. I refused to give him an easy go at that life. I refused to let how I felt or fears I had rule over what I needed to do (or *not* do) for him. Elliot is living proof that there is great hope for those in the death grip of the plague that is sweeping the nation, destroying families and taking lives.

Annie's Message: Nothing I could ever do, say, think, or feel will keep my son sober. I can direct and advise him. I can do the right things in order to not participate and therefore cause him to face life without being enabled in it. But I cannot cause, control or cure my son's problems with substances or anything else! His life, health and well-being are up to him; mine are up to me.

ROUND ELEVEN

My Favorite Word

Some people are going to be happy with my decision and some people aren't. I just have to live my life. —Tommy Hearns

Equanimity: A calm mental state, especially after a shock or disappointment or in a difficult situation.[1]

I AM THE MOTHER OF AN ADDICT. I am in recovery as much as my addicted son is in recovery.

Like many who hear about or personally experience the destructive effects of addiction, it took serious convincing for me to consider it a "disease." In fact, I was pretty self-righteous about it. I told myself *you don't see a cancer patient or diabetic stealing from the jewelry box of a family member, or damaging the people that love and need them.* But I didn't have an informed understanding of addiction. I was certain I could outsmart and tough love my son right out of addiction. I was the sharp-tongued, correct-handling, consequence-forcing, perfect *model* of a non-enabler. So I was a very hard sell about addiction as a disease, yet I have come to believe my son's addiction is a disease and I am powerless over it.

Similar to how someone diagnosed with a heart condition

needs to make serious lifestyle changes, an addict must renovate their entire life and everything about how they manage it in order to arrest and recover from the diseased thinking and cravings of addiction. It began with the choice to pick up their particular substance the first time or two. Brain chemistry changes once someone becomes gripped, and that is often innocently done based on injury or falling under influence. It can and it does happen to anyone. I have learned that once brain chemistry becomes diseased it then causes the desperation and craving to bypass their love of family and often their own ethics. People raised to know better can become desperate and criminal, needing their next fix as much as their lungs need oxygen. It is only the person who is addicted that can choose the road to recovery. We can affect that path, but we cannot control it. I have never understood this truth more than after witnessing a relapse.

My son went into recovery three years ago, but had two relapse setbacks, each with a worse set of circumstances. Once we start to get our lives back on track after addiction hits a family and the addict begins to recover, a relapse can feel more crushing than when you found out they were addicted to begin with. We hope they have sobered up once and forever. I have realized that relapses are a part of recovery and that the addiction is not about me. It is not a personal attack on me. It is about the fact that the disease is chronic and recovery has to be consistent and taken serious. I have also realized that if we all live through it and the consequences aren't too damaging, so much can be learned.

~

For after all, the best thing one can do when it's raining is let it rain. —Henry Wadsworth Longfellow

The most valuable thing I learned is how to separate my peace of mind and detach my well-being from the roller coaster of chaos that is par for the course with addiction. Sure there will be triggers and it's all quite painful and terrifying. But I don't have to live and dwell in the ups and downs or run alongside the craziness of anyone else's choices. In the midst of my son's relapse, I stepped out of the storm. I found my own peace and serenity.

I discovered what became my favorite word: **Equanimity.** I compare equanimity to trying to do a quiet activity like read, sew or meditate while a loud jackhammer tears up the sidewalk outside your window. I had to learn how to calm myself and separate from the noise and chaos as it was happening. It is possible! But it takes decision and discipline.

I had always found that when my son would call me in a panic over problems or stress, my mind would begin to triage his issues for him, almost like a reflex. Instead of considering the fact that maybe I'm not *supposed* to handle it. Very counter-intuitive for a parent! But when you are dealing with the disease of addiction, life has to be handled completely different. We can't jump into the stress with them.

You can love someone without taking on their problems. You don't have to be pinned against the ropes with them.

After the relapse, I went to classes again and learned more ways of handling my role as the mom of an addict. One great method I use when stress erupts and I need to stop and calm myself is a breathing exercise. I remind myself to turn to my breath for a moment. I take a step back in the midst and inhale a four-count breath, hold it for two counts and exhale it for four counts. I do this five or six times. This breathing technique floods peace and oxygen to my extremities and sets my brain on neutral just long enough that I don't rush into madness with anyone. If I'm still surging with adrenaline, I will take a walk alone or with my dog before I allow myself to react or make any decisions.

Another thing I learned after Elliot's relapse was to fully lean on the "3 C's" of Al-Anon:

1. We didn't **Cause** it
2. We can't **Control** it and
3. We can't **Cure** it. To expand on those:

Cause: At this point blaming who, what, where, why and how the addiction started or why relapse occurred is futile. This train of thought only adds to the misery and distracts from handling it in functional, healthy ways. This pertains to past, present as much as potential substance abuse. I can't live in fear that by saying/doing the wrong thing I will send him spiraling back into the cycle. I am not the cause of that. Someone who wants to remain clean will do so regardless of stress or pressure. There will always be stress and pressure! The key is learning to cope without abusing a substance. And that is up to them to develop. Emotionally tiptoeing around someone won't prevent substance abuse any more than bulldozing and bullying will. Working a program is the way forward. I take care of myself. My priority is to make sure *I'm* healthy and functional. My health and wellness helps my son choose health and wellness. Participating in the dynamics of his addiction does not.

Control: Policing and making sure they are going to meetings, spending time with sober companions, doing what they are supposed to should only be something paid attention to for your own safety and boundaries. Taking control of their life, recovery or participating in the craziness as it occurs is not healthy for anyone.

Cure: Nothing I can do, say, think, or feel will heal or cure it. I can affect his decisions with healthy boundaries, prayer and faith, by not enabling or participating. And by taking care of myself. Other than that . . . it is up to him to want it, to work a program, and to recover.

Annie's Message: When most recovered addicts are asked what led to their sobriety, they will often run through a list of very difficult circumstances: Getting arrested, going to jail, an overdose, the death of someone close to them from an overdose, being hungry, homeless and losing everyone that cares about them. You won't hear a list of things their mom or dad did to help and comfort them, nor who helped pay drug dealers to get them off their back, who took them in, gave them clothes, money, a shower, etc. Hard times and consequences are the only way they come to hate their lives on their own and take the step toward treatment and sobriety. I was able to parry the trajectory, but I couldn't live every moment of every situation for him. Not a single one! To this day, Elliot tells me two of the greatest gifts I ever gave him were misery and desperation.

ROUND TWELVE

Annie

It's not the size of the man but the size of his heart that matters.
—Evander Holyfield

Self-care: The maintenance of one's personal well-being and health. A necessary human regulatory function, which is under individual control, deliberate and self-initiated.
Functional: Designed for or capable of a particular function or use.[1]
Serenity: The state of being peaceful, untroubled. Calm, clearness.[2]
Sophrosyne: A healthy state of mind, characterized by self-control, moderation and a deep awareness of one's true self resulting in true happiness.

ELLIOT AND I BOTH went through recovery. Simultaneously, yet separately. He turned his life back over to treatment and recovery. I found individual peace and equanimity in the eye of his storm. I wholly accept the truth that I can no more control his decisions, navigate his life or prevent his death when it comes to addiction than I can control him getting into a fatal car accident. All I can do is live gratefully and peacefully within each day; I can be the best me I can be, and have a healthy relationship with my son and anyone else in my life. It is up to Elliot to choose the same. And that is relief beyond words! My son is clean and sober again, doing the work on and for himself. That could change again. But I refuse to live in the fear of it. I choose, instead, to live in peace and in the present.

I don't harbor hard feelings toward my mother or anyone else. That would hinder how much life has for me. If I rehearse the negatives—the hurt, disappointments, the damages—how would I see the beauty and the blessings?

~

Learning to walk again . . . —Foo Fighters

I LOVE and cherish my son. I want him happy, healthy and OLD! But I am not the author, creator or controller of life. I am not the Higher Power by any means, nor do I get to call the shots when it comes to how it unfolds. My son's life and recovery may not play out like I expect. In fact, most of life doesn't go according to my exact plans! I've made peace with that. The main event for me was coming to a place where I believe detaching from his decisions was okay for a mother. That is where I remember to let my faith take over versus my fear.

At one time, I thought the happy ending of our story was how "Elliot's Mom" who spent twenty years researching behavioral science, took a strong, healthy, non-enabling approach to his addiction and *caused* him to get sober and live well. Now I know nothing could be further from the truth. Even my "healthy," strong tactics couldn't save him. I was still enmeshed and participating! I may have helped direct him toward sobriety, but I had no power over it otherwise.

The relapse part of our story puts to rest both blame or heroic rescue having any control over my child's painful addiction. I had tried every possible textbook method and beyond, yet still, I was not able to cause, control or cure his way left or right! I didn't cause it, I can't control it and I will never cure it. I can only contribute in healthy (or unhealthy) ways and I can cope with it. Elliot has to choose recovery for himself and *that* is when recovery works. The stronger and healthier I am, the better chance he has of choosing healthy for himself.

And so finally, with a healthy, un-enmeshed relationship with my son, instead of always answering to "Elliot's Mom," you can call me Annie.

Non Deficere! **(*Never give up!*)**

∼

Only a man who knows what it's like to be defeated can reach
down to the bottom of his soul and come up with the extra
ounce of power it takes to win when the match is even.
—Muhammad Ali

Afterword

IT TOOK SOME TIME for me to adapt to the calm after the storm. For a while I had somewhat of a glass jaw. Everything triggered post stress for me. I was easily frustrated, made afraid or angry. It took time to calm down and relax into that calm.

You sometimes don't know what to do with yourself once a daily threat is removed. Once life settled down. I had to settle down! I had to make peace within rather than allowing outside forces to pull me along into stress and strife whenever the wind blew.

When you are used to the chaos and eruptions of crises, you have to recalibrate your brain to settle into a routine of quiet and peace. I had to choose to be careful and mindful about it and to remain aware of those things that caused me to feel upset and chaotic. At times, when it was quiet, I caught myself searching for something upsetting! That was all part of the aftermath and it eventually went away.

It takes time to layer down through the damages to come to a calm place where you trust life again. But it will happen, particularly when you do the work to heal and recover.

In the boxing world, Elliot would be considered the purse. He is the prize I was fighting for! I could dig deep for confidence to fight for him. And now I fight for me! I fight for peace, serenity and what is right—but in a soft way. My fight approach is more stylist than anything, but if at all possible, I'd rather not engage conflict.

You have to be a pretty worthy opponent to get me into the arena of conflict. I'm more likely to walk away from upset now in my daily pursuit of peace and joy.

∽

I will not walk backward in life. —J.R.R. Tolkien

I decided not to live anymore as the neglected, uncared for little girl, nor would I carry the identity of a disconnected, rebellious, polarizing teenager and young mother. I let go of walking with the limp of a mother of a son deep in distress. Instead, I chose peace, strength and courage.

What does life feel like now? We talk about mundane things and it doesn't hurt like they are being discussed in the presence of a wound. Holidays, vacations, 5Ks and fitness goals . . . all things we plan on and discuss with excitement and joy! Life feels normal, but different. Forever changed, but somehow better for it all. I wouldn't change the bitter lessons we went through. I wouldn't undo our hard times for what they taught us, how they deepened us and where they led us.

But I never want to live those days again!

Every day I tell myself I have survived and I will continue to do so. No matter what could happen tomorrow, no matter what could fall apart, I am okay today. I have a crystal clear understanding that life can drop you to your knees in a moment. Without notice! And when that happens, don't expect a pass from anything or anyone. When you find yourself there, breathe, pray and figure out moment-to-moment how you are going to survive to live out your story with grit and character.

Then get up swingin'.

~

Trials will either prove your credibility or they will create it. I believe treasures are buried for us to discover within every fiery trial. Deep truth, conquering fears, building, faith and finding love and confidence for yourself can all emerge from the darkest valley. How you handle trials gives you credibility and honor once you come through them . . . once you clear the "until" phase of them.

Annie's Message: I'm not trying to shame anyone, make anyone feel bad about themselves, or feel sorry for me. For the most part, people do the best they can with the tools that have. I went on to accomplish great things and much as to make terrible mistakes. I hold nothing against anyone, I blame the good and the bad of my life on no one but myself. Plenty of people have been through much worse! I simply hope to share my experiences. What happens in each of our lives can break you or fortify you . . . the decision is ours. What was meant for my hard, instead worked together with Synergeo perfection to fortify me.

~

Whenever I allowed myself to slip into anger, to relive the unfair, pain-filled moments and slide into bitterness I'd then lose the joyful feeling of hope for my goals and dreams. It would disappear in the darkness of negativity. We can't have both. I learned to let hard feelings come but then go—painful memories come and go. I learned to let it all come and *flow* and pass on through me. Letting it all go allowed me keep on believing daily for the greatest good and reaching for the best life possible.

My relationship with Elliot today is healthy, jovial and loving. He is still a great joy to my heart! My relationship with my son is somewhat of a "corner coach." His recovery is his own; he, too, has a path to travel. I can encourage, advise, console and inform. I can say "Get back in the fight!" or "Take a breath and sit this one out," but I cannot control his life or create his outcomes, nor do I have the desire to.

Where is my relationship with my mother today? I have made peace. I forgive all of it. I wish her peace, joy and much emotional freedom and well-being. I do not wish for her to live even one day in shame or regret.

My relationship with family is healthier; we are all a work in progress and each has their own journey to traverse. Realizing that makes it easier to extend acceptance. People do the best they can with the tools they have.

My relationship with those who were a disappointing or painful part of my journey is also forgiveness. But I would say, you never know what despair someone is burdened with as you encounter them on the mundane avenues of daily life. Show kindness, always, because, to quote Ram Dass, "We are all just walking each other home."

During the worst of times, during the mean-times, as well as when things were amazing, these are the daily goals I focused my attention and energy on:

1. Peace of mind, emotional wellbeing, spiritual, mental wellness.

2. Meditations, prayer, breathing, spiritual practices and calming methods, etc. This one also includes my research of behavioral science and functionality. Workshops, "Ted Talks" books, and classes.

3. Physical health and fitness.

4. Wellness shots, smoothies, vitamins, exercise, water and walks..

5. Work responsibilities.

6. Work hard in the job that pays the bills!

7. Goals, hopes, dreams.

Whatever it is that reigns with passion in your heart to become, to do . . . take steps toward it daily!

8. Relational – family, friendships, relationships with those close to me

Only allow people close who are supportive, kind, FAIR, loving and who are rooting for you. And vice versa. Do something daily to encourage that, to uplift them . . . to keep the connections healthy! Allow them to do for you as well. And sometimes – healthy means boundaries and distance. Whatever it takes for positive connections in the closest relationships in your life

Goals will keep you on track, save you from getting stuck in a rut, pull you out of conflict and drama, keep you from petty concerns . . . and before you know it, your life is rising! You can come out of every season of life not only ahead in these goal areas, but with results chasing you! The best response or react to any negative, the best counterpunch to any time of crisis *is accomplishing goals!*

Acknowledgments

Special thanks to . . .

My Creator, Counselor, Confidante, Comforter, Advocate, Defense, Helper, Healer, Father, Functionality, Strength, Support, Rescuer, Confidence, Courage, the Alpha and Omega, to it all, through it all, my everything! The source of all life, love, hope and well-being, my Higher Power. Because You exist, because I am Yours and in Your care, I can face it all. The unfolding of Your plans for me by far surpasses my dreams for my own life! I swing for the fence and You launch it to the moon. My heart is grateful to You first, foremost and forevermore.

Dad, you spoke so much into my life that has echoed years beyond your passing. Your grit lives on within me and is being handed on again and again. You taught me to keep moving, versus settling into a hard thing long enough to feel sorry for myself. Adversity is a launch pad; problems are projects, and life is a flowing current. In my weakest moments, your voice would come to mind inspiring me to get up and go on. Had it not been for you, I would have lost the will to live in the midst of the many battles. Because of *you*, no matter what—come hell or high water—I rise.

Mom, if we both hadn't failed miserably, I would have never come to know my own strength. I would have never learned to trust and believe in myself, and I would have never gone for it. Because of you, I learned to write and poured my heart out in a stack of journals. Because of you, I found and pursued my passion, releasing and expressing all things through words. Because of you, I swung for the fence! If it all had not been, this would not be.

Mom and Dad, you *both* gave me a love and a passion for writing and for reading books, a passion that has absolutely sustained and carried me through life! You have my deepest gratitude.

My son, the joy of my life, the thorn in my side, and my reason through it all. You know your worth to me! It goes far beyond words.

Jeff, we hit many hurdles and hardships through the years—some painful, painful days! During the worst of them, when life was falling apart and felt totally ungrounded, I have to say you are the one who cheered me on and helped me to keep going. You kept rooting for me when it looked impossible—maybe even stupid—for me to continue, whether it was a fight for the best outcome, or the decision to share our story in the midst of so much crisis. Your support was consistent and ever-present. You stuck by me and showed up when I felt most alone and sat with me through the long periods of silent waiting. When solutions would finally come, you were as relieved as if it were your story. You came to my door with a printer when mine gave up on me. You sent me articles, ideas, and suggestions daily. You have been a constant thread of belief in me. The telling of our story would not have continued if it were not for your support. I am forever in your debt and I love you beyond words. You are family.

Greg Hannley and the SOBA Recovery Center, you literally saved the life of my son. More than once! You are precious and dear to me. Your long-term help, love and support are life changing for our family.

Denise and Six Degrees Publishing, my heart is forever grateful to you for taking a chance on me. For the patience and grace you have handled me with, it goes without saying that you are the biggest reason I was able to put my heart on the page and have it brought to life.

Barb, my teacher and encourager in those early years of struggle. Thank you for illuminating the path I would walk toward. You were lifesaving.

Wally, what a friend you were. I treasure our conversations in my memory and sort through them often. I miss you so very much and will carry the memory of your sweet, fun soul alive with me until we meet again.

Jennifer, my laughter and my relief! Had it not been for you my heart would have failed! The inside jokes, sleeping on my couch so I wouldn't wake up alone and afraid; listening for hours as I'd lament and moan over every torment. You are more priceless to me than you will ever know! "It ain't over yet; the best is yet to come!" I couldn't live without you.

Jim, you should have been given an honorary therapist's degree by now for the hours you sat on the phone letting me pour my life out in excruciating detail. I believe we started that at fifteen! I am so thankful to have you in every phase of life. Someone like you comes along once in a lifetime and only to the luckiest of people. No one can compete with your loyalty. Our best memories are still to come. I am more than grateful to be going through life with you.

Scott, thank you for being the best ex-husband imaginable! Our unity and friendship was lifesaving as we sorted through these terrible times. You were a great support—sometimes a pain in every way and always annoying—but, I wouldn't trade you for anyone.

Greg, my brother-in-law, friend, teacher and all around helper in every way possible. I would take you into any battle! I am so grateful to have you in the family.

Pam, I learned so much, so fast from you! You came along just in time. The boundaries class you taught and the behavioral science workshops you took me to: life changing! Mothering me, showing up: it is all treasured and gave me strength to fight on. You untangled me in so many ways—from so many dysfunctional things—teaching me the two types of wisdom: One coming from someone who seems to be for you, but will sting you eventually because it's self-serving and has a selfish agenda; the other wisdom giving peace, relief and shedding light into dark places where knowledge didn't exist. I am not as easily fooled by the former, and I am more open to the latter because of you! I am forever in your debt! My heart and my sanity thank you eternally.

Teresa, thank you for meeting with me weekly to hear my sorrow and worry. Your words still ring in my heart.

Cindy, you are special to me!

Kim W.C., ever-present, always getting it…there at the hardest moments no matter how unbearable.

Jamie, your friendship is worth its weight in gold. So many times, I considered giving in and letting the grief and night terrors swallow me up, but you come through with a right-on-time reminder to *just . . . keep . . . going.* You will always hold a special place in my life!

Chris, you were a big, protective brother so many times. Quick to make me laugh and to ask about our circumstances *regularly*. I am so thankful for you!

Holly, my leaning post! How on earth did you stand me? I was always sure I would drain you completely with my daily analyzing in the worst of these times. You were calm, reassuring and one of the greatest comforts I've ever known.

Tiff, my sister in every way except biologically. You have my loyalty forever.

Jill, my encourager, my friend and adopted sister. You can never get out of that role!

Heather, you came to the fight late, but you are as special to me as is anyone; I am so very thankful for you!

Amy, coworker, friend and confidante. I came to love you so fast! You are just that kind.

Kim: You showed up in a day of extreme suffering and gave me so much encouragement. I will be thankful for you for eternity; you can do no wrong in my sight!

My family, you taught me a great deal—when I succeed, you succeed.

Nar-Anon support groups, who were a source of comfort, information and empathy.

Parkside Treatment Center, who allowed me to meet with families and share my story of success (and failures) and hope!

Friends who came and went, who came and sat—impromptu strength and encouragement from those of you in passing, I remember every detail! I am grateful for you.

Coworkers who were patient, understanding and sympathetic anytime I was extremely on edge and needed to take a breath, I remember all of you, and I am grateful.

Signs of Addiction [1]

Substance dependence - when a person is addicted to a substance, such as a drug, alcohol or nicotine, they are not able to control the use of that substance. They continue taking it, even though it may cause harm (the individual may or may not be aware of the potential harm).

Substance dependence can cause powerful cravings. The addict may want to give up (quit), but finds it extremely difficult to do so without help.

The signs and symptoms of substance dependence vary according to the individual, the substance they are addicted to, their family history (genetics), and personal circumstances.

Signs and symptoms of substance addiction may include:

-The person takes the substance and cannot stop - in many cases, such as nicotine, alcohol or drug dependence, at least one serious attempt was made to give up, but unsuccessfully.

-Withdrawal symptoms - when body levels of that substance go below a certain level the patient has physical and mood-related symptoms. There are cravings, bouts of moodiness, bad temper, poor focus, a feeling of being depressed and empty, frustration, anger, bitterness and resentment.

There may suddenly be increased appetite. Insomnia is a common symptom of withdrawal. In some cases the individual may have constipation or diarrhea. Withdrawal can trigger violence, trembling, seizures, hallucinations, and sweats.

-**Addiction continues despite health problem awareness** - the individual continues taking the substance regularly, even though they have developed illnesses linked to it. For example, a smoker may continue smoking even after a lung or heart condition develops.

-**Social and/or recreational sacrifices** - some activities are given up because of an addiction to something. For example, an alcoholic may turn down an invitation to go camping or spend a day out on a boat if no alcohol is available, a smoker may decide not to meet up with friends in a smoke-free pub or restaurant.

-**Maintaining a good supply** - people who are addicted to a substance will always make sure they have a good supply of it, even if they do not have much money. Sacrifices may be made in the house budget to make sure the substance is as plentiful as possible.

-**Taking risks (1)** - in some cases the addicted individual may take risks to make sure he/she can obtain his/her substance, such as stealing or trading sex for money/drugs.

-**Taking risks (2)** - while under the influence of some substances the addict may engage in risky activities, such as driving fast.

-**Dealing with problems** - an addicted person commonly feels they need their drug to deal with their problems.

-**Obsession** - an addicted person may spend more and more time and energy focusing on ways of getting hold of their substance, and in some cases how to use it.

-**Secrecy and solitude** - in many cases the addict may take their substance alone, and even in secret.

-**Denial** - a significant number of people who are addicted to a substance are in denial. They are not aware (or refuse to acknowledge) that they have a problem.

-**Excess consumption** - in some addictions, such as alcohol, some drugs and even nicotine, the individual consumes it to excess. The consequence can be blackouts (cannot remember chunks of time) or physical symptoms, such as a sore throat and bad persistent cough (heavy smokers).

–**Dropping hobbies and activities** - as the addiction progresses the individual may stop doing things he/she used to enjoy a lot. This may even be the case with smokers who find they cannot physically cope with taking part in their favorite sport.

–**Having stashes** - the addicted individual may have small stocks of their substance hidden away in different parts of the house or car; often in unlikely places.

–**Taking an initial large dose** - this is common with alcoholism. The individual may gulp drinks down in order to get drunk and then feel good.

–**Having problems with the law** - this is more a characteristic of some drug and alcohol addictions (not nicotine, for example). This may be either because the substance impairs judgment and the individual takes risks they would not take if they were sober, or in order to get hold of the substance they break the law.

–**Financial difficulties** - if the substance is expensive the addicted individual may sacrifice a lot to make sure its supply is secured. Even cigarettes, which in some countries, such as the UK, parts of Europe and the USA cost over $11 for a packet of 20—a 40-a-day smoker in such an area will need to put aside $660 per month, nearly $8,000 per year.

–**Relationship problems** - these are more common in drug/alcohol addiction.

~

"If they can make penicillin out of moldy bread, then they can sure make something out of you." —Muhammad Ali

Boxing terms[1]

Accidental Butt: When the heads of both fighters just so happen to collide during the course of a fight. No one is ruled responsible in such a case.

Alphabet Groups: Term used to describe the numerous boxing organizations (WBA, IBF, WBC, WBO) that govern the sport.

Bleeder: A fighter who is vulnerable to cuts.

Bob and Weave: When a fighter moves his upper body in an up-and-down motion, making him more difficult to time correctly.

Bolo Punch: A showy, sweeping punch that looks like a little like an uppercut. More of a showboating tactic.

Bout: Another word for a boxing match.

Brawler: An aggressive fighter who likes to fight on the inside.

Break: The moment when the fighters are separating from a clinch.

Buckle: When fighter's legs give way, as in "that punched buckled him."

Canvas: The floor in a boxing ring.

Card: The list of fights happening in a single boxing event.

Caught Cold: Term used to describe a fighter knocked out early in the fight who was not mentally prepared or warmed up properly.

Chief Second: The head trainer in charge of a fighter's corner.

Clinch: When fighters hold each other.

Combination: A seamless sequence of consecutive punches.

Contender: A fighter in a position to perhaps challenge for a championship.

Corkscrew Punch: A punch thrown in a twisting motion, which often causes cuts.

Cornerman: One of several people who work in a fighter's corner during a fight.

Counterpunch: Punch thrown in response to another fighter's attack.

Covering Up: Defensive tactic where a fighter goes into a shell to thwart his opponent's offensive.

Cross: Power punch thrown straight with the rear hand.

Cutman: Cornerman responsible for tending to swelling and cuts.

Dive: When a fighter purposely loses.

Eight Count: After a fighter is knocked down, the referee must complete a count of eight even if the opponent rises before that.

Enswell: Piece of cold metal that is pressed on swelling to prevent the eyes from closing.

Faded: Term used to describe a fighter past his peak powers.

Feint: When a fighter acts like he's going to punch but does not in order to get his opponent to react.

Flash knockdown: When a fighter is briefly knocked down, more as a result of a surprise or happenstance than being seriously hurt.

Fringe Contender: Low-rated contender on the cusp of the world rankings.

Gate: Total amount of money generated from ticket sales.

Gatekeeper: Term used to describe a fighter who is not a threat to be champion, but opponents can establish themselves as a legitimate contender by beating him.

Get Off: A fighter's ability to get his offense untracked.

Glass Jaw: A trait of a fighter with questionable punch-resistance.

Go the Distance: Lasting for the complete scheduled duration of a fight.

Go to the Body: A strategy that centers on trying to deplete an opponents' resolve by repeatedly punching to the body and not so much the head.

Go to the Cards: When the judges decide who won a fight that either went the distance or was stopped prematurely.

Governing Body: An organization that sanctions fights.

Haymaker: A wild punch intended to knock out the opponent.

Infighting: Close-range boxing.

Journeyman: A skilled fighter, while not necessarily a winning one. Used as opponents and to test up and coming boxers. They lack meaningful connections and take fights on short notice.

Kidney Punch: Illegal body punch thrown to the rear area of an opponent's body.

Liver Shot: Legal punch when a left hook connects with the lower right side of an opponent's body with devastating effect.

Low Blow: Punch deemed by the referee to be below the legal level.

Main Event: The most important fight on a card.

Mauler: An inside fighter who tries to prevail by smothering his opponents.

Majority Decision: When two judges agree a certain fighter won, while the third judge scores it as a draw.

Mouse: An isolated and protruding swelling on a fighter's face.

Neutral Corner: One of two unoccupied corners in the ring and where fighters are sent after they knock down their opponents.

No-Decision: When a fight has no win-lose-draw result, usually from an early-rounds cut or an extenuating circumstance that does not allow a fight to finish.

On the Ropes: Term used to describe a fighter in a dangerous situation trapped with his back against the ropes in a boxing ring.

Orthodox: Describes a right-handed fighter.

Outside Fighter: Boxer that prefers operating from long-range.

Palooka: Term used to describe an aging, losing, or uncelebrated boxer.

Parry: Changing the trajectory of an opponent's punch using the gloves to slap away the shot.

Paw: To meekly poke a jab out.

Play Possum: To act hurt in an effort to get an opponent to over-commit.

Plodder: A slow-footed fighter with no agility.

Point Deduction: When a foul or series of fouls warrant a one-point penalty, the equivalent of losing a round.

Pound-for-Pound: Term created to rank fighters based on excellence and not weight.

Puncher's Chance: When an under-skilled, but hard-hitting fighter must rely solely on his punching power to win a fight.

Purse: The money a fighter earns for a given fight.

Queer Street: State of a fighter who does not have full control of his faculties after taking punishment.

Rabbit Punch: An illegal punch to the back of the head.

Ring Generalship: When a fighter is controlling and dictating the fight. When one fighter is imposing his will on the fight more than his opponent.

Ringside: A position that is close to the ring.

Roll with the Punches: When an opponent bends and twists with the punch, minimizing its impact.

Rope-a-Dope: Allowing an opponent to go on the offensive while covering up on the ropes and waiting for him to tire.

Roughhousing: When an opponent fights in an overly physical and unruly way.

Rubber Match: When opponents fight for a third time, each having won one bout apiece.

Sanctioning Body: A group that organizes world title bouts.

Saved by the Bell: When a round ends, saving a hurt fighter that was on the verge of being knocked out.

Second: A cornerman.

Shopworn: A fighter who is slowing down after a long career.

Slip: To move the head slightly to avoid a punch.

Southpaw: A left-handed fighter.

Spar: Boxing for practice.

Split Draw: When two judges disagree on who won a fight, while the third judge has it a draw.

Stablemate: Fighters who train at the same gym or under the banner of the same promoter.

Stick and Move: Technique when a fighter moves around the ring fighting only at long range.

Stylist: A fighter who relies on skills rather than brawn.

Sucker Punch: A punch thrown at a distracted or otherwise unprepared opponent.

Titlist: Fighter who holds one of the many available "world" title belts, but is not recognized as the true or linear champion.

Technical Decision: When a bout is terminated prematurely due to a cut or some other circumstance sending the bout to the scorecards.

Technical Draw: When a bout is ended prematurely and the scoring is even.

Technical Knockout: When a fighter is taking too much punishment and the referee stops the bout without completing a ten-count.

Throw in the Towel: When the chief second in a fighter's corner wants to stop the fight, he throws a towel into the ring.

Toe-to-Toe: When both fighters stand in front of each other and engage.

Trialhorse: Capable but largely unsuccessful opponent used to gauge if other fighters are ready to make a jump in class.

Undercard: Series of fights that take place before the main event.

Upstart: A new fighter with potential.

Walkout Bout: A low-caliber fight at the end of a fight card.

Whiskers: Chin. Used to describe a fighter's durability, as in "he has a good set of whiskers."

Notes & References

Introduction

1. *Webster's New Collegiate Dictionary* G. & C. Merriam Co (1973).
2. https://en.oxforddictionaries.com/definition/codependency (Retrieved September 26, 2016).
3. http://www.dictionary.com/browse/dysfunction (Retrieved September 26, 2016).
4. http://www.merriam-webster.com/dictionary/enabler (Retrieved September 26 ,2016).
5. http://www.dictionary.com/browse/family?s=t accessed (Retrieved September 26, 2016).
6. http://www.merriam-webster.com/dictionary/peace (Retrieved September 26, 2016).
7. http://www.merriam-webster.com/dictionary/well-being (Retrieved September 26, 2016).
8. Increases in Heroin Overdose Deaths — 28 States, 2010 to 2012 *Weekly* October 3, 2014 / 63(39);849-854 www.cdc.gov/mmwr/preview/mmwrhtml/mm6339a1.htm (Retrieved August 30,2016).
9. Examples of opioids are: Painkillers such as; morphine, methadone, Buprenorphine, hydrocodone, and oxycodone. Heroin is also an opioid and is illegal. Opioid drugs sold under brand names include: OxyContin®, Percocet®, Palladone® (taken off the market 7/2005),Vicodin®, Percodan®, Tylox® andDemerol® among others. https://www.naabt.org/faq_answers.cfm?ID=4 (Retrieved September 26 2016).

Round One

1. *Strong's Exhaustive Concordance, The Strongest Strong* (Michigan: Zondervan, 2001).

Round Two

1. *Strong's Exhaustive Concordance, The Strongest Strong* (Michigan: Zondervan, 2001).
2. https://en.oxforddictionaries.com/definition/rebellion (Retrieved September 26, 2016).
3. http://www.merriam-webster.com/medical/thanatophobia (Retrieved September 26, 2016)
4. Easy bleeders is a boxing term. (*see Appendix B* of this book)

Round Three

1. https://en.oxforddictionaries.com/definition/charisma (Retrieved (September 26, 2016).

2. http://www.merriam-webster.com/dictionary/charisma (Retrieved September 26, 2016).

3. http://sv.urbandictionary.com/define.php?term=charisma (Retrieved September 26, 2016).

Round Four

1. http://www.dictionary.com/browse/conflict (Retrieved September 26, 2016).

2. http://www.dictionary.com/browse/enmeshed (Retrieved September 26, 2016).

3. http://www.dictionary.com/browse/enmeshed (Retrieved September 26, 2016).

(4) http://www.dictionary.com/browse/individuate (Retrieved September 26 2016).

(5) https://en.oxforddictionaries.com/definition/vicissitude (Retrieved September 26, 2016).

Round Five

1. http://www.dictionary.com/browse/obsess (Retrieved September 26, 2016).

2. http://www.dictionary.com/browse/persevere (Retrieved September 27, 2016).

3. http://www.merriam-webster.com/dictionary/ruminate (Retrieved September 27, 2016).

Round Six

1. http://www.merriam-webster.com/dictionary/chaos (Retrieved September 27, 2016).

2. http://www.merriam-webster.com/dictionary/misery (Retrieved September 27, 2016).

3. "False" used here means "unchristian," or not acting in a Christian-like manner according to church teachings.

Round Seven

1. http://www.dictionary.com/browse/turmoil (Retrieved September 27, 2016).

Round Eight

1. http://www.merriam-webster.com/dictionary/uncertainty (Retrieved

September 27, 2016).

Round Nine

1. *Random House Kernerman Webster's College Dictionary.* (2010). (Retrieved September 27, 2016) from http://www.thefreedictionary. com/detach.

2. http://www.merriam-webster.com/dictionary/surrender (Retrieved September 27, 2016).

Round Ten

1. http://www.merriam-webster.com/dictionary/relapse (Retrieved September 27, 2016).

2. http://www.dictionary.com/browse/renovate (Retrieved September 27, 2016).

3. http://www.merriam-webster.com/dictionary/restore (Retrieved September 27, 2016).

4. restore. (n.d.) *American Heritage® Dictionary of the English Language, Fifth Edition.* (2011). (Retrieved September 27, 2016) from http://www. thefreedictionary.com/.

Round Eleven

1. http://dictionary.cambridge.org/dictionary/English/equanimity (Retrieved September 27 2016).

Round Twelve

1. *American Heritage® Dictionary of the English Language, Fifth Edition.* (2011). (Retrieved September 27 2016) from http://thedictionary.com/ functional.

2. http://www.dictionary.com/browse/serenity.

Appendix A

1. "Signs of Addiction" from Medical News Today Blog http://www. medicalnewstoday.com/info/addiction/signs-of-addiction.php (Retrieved October 6,2016).

Appendix B

1. "Basic Boxing Vocabulary" from Flashdecks.com http://flashdecks. com/node/265/export (retrieved September 27, 2016).

Annie's Suggested Reading & Links

INSPIRATIONAL BOOKS:

Brene Brown, *Rising Strong* (Spiegel & Grau, 2015)
Iyania Vanzant, *In the Meantime* (Simon & Schuster, 2015)
Iyania Vanzant, *Trust* (Smiley Books, 2015)
Beth Moore, *Stepping Up* (Lifeway Press, 2007)
Gavom de Becler, *The Gift of Fear* (Gavin de Becker, 2010)
George Foreman, *God in My Corner* (Thomas Nelson, 2007)
Jewel, *Never Broken* (Blue Rider Press, 2016)
Barbara Johnson:
> *When Your Child Breaks Your Heart* (Revell, 2008)
> *Boomerang Joy* (Zondervan, 1998)
> *Stick a Geranium in Your Hat and Be Happy* (Thomas Nelson, 2004)

LINKS TO HELPFUL ARTICLES:

How can I tell if I am being manipulated?

"14 Signs of Psychological and Emotional Manipulation"
by Preston Ni, M.S.B.A.
https://www.psychologytoday.com/blog/communication-success/201510/14-signs-psychological-and-emotional-manipulation

How can I tell if I am being lied to?

"15 Signs that the Person You're Dating is Lying to You"
by Megan Willet
http://www.businessinsider.com/15-signs-that-youre-being-lied-to-2013-2

Codependency

"Patterns and Characteristics of Codepence" by Coda.Org
http://coda.org/index.cfm/meeting-materials1/patterns-and-
characteristics-2011/

How do I not enable?

"How Do I Stop Enabling My Grown-Up Child"
by Elements Behavioral Health
https://www.elementsbehavioralhealth.com/addiction/how-to-
stop-enabling-your-grown-up-child/

When you are feeling crazy

"What 'Am I Crazy?' Really Means" by Katherine Kim for WebMD
http://www.webmd.com/mental-health/features/am-i-crazy